S0-AYC-599

Saul W. Gellerman
Managers and
Subordinates

Saul W. Gellerman

Managers and
Subordinates

The Dryden Press
Hinsdale, Illinois

Copyright © 1976 by the Dryden Press
A Division of Holt, Rinehart and Winston
All rights reserved
Library of Congress Catalog Card Number: 76–385
ISBN: 0–03–089928–1
Printed in the United States of America
7 8 9   065   9 8 7 6 5 4 3 2

175430

658.3
G 318 ma

Material in Chapter Three, entitled
Supervisors and Productivity, has
been adapted and published in the
March-April 1976 issue of *Harvard
Business Review*

For Fred McKinney,
who had faith in me
thirty years ago

Preface

I do not believe that the economic problems of this world can be solved by machines or by money. Our problems are the result of the ways in which political leaders have managed economies, labor leaders have managed unions, and business leaders have managed companies. Briefly, we have managed our way into our problems, and it is only with better management—and, therefore, better managers—that we can hope to manage our way out.

Not that capital is unimportant. Obviously, it is indispensable; but unless capital is related intelligently to the people who must operate and care for it, its usefulness is rapidly and steeply degraded. Sophisticated, expensive equipment in the hands of hostile or de-motivated workers is no more productive, in the long run, than the antiquated equipment it has replaced.

Thus there is no escape from the age-old problem of intelligently managing people. We have computers, lasers, and the other paraphernalia of advanced technology; but the people who must operate and care for them still have egos, IQs, and in many cases all the psychological equivalents of pimples—just as they have had for centuries. For some reason unknown to us, God did not choose to make any of us as logical, simple, or perfect as we can make a machine.

Therefore the core problem of management remains what it has always been: accomplishing productive work by organizing and motivating the efforts of other people. Since mankind has shown no recent signs of evolving any more rapidly than it has in the past toward amenability to being told what to do, we must conclude that for the foreseeable future, people will remain difficult to supervise.

What I have tried to do in this book is to distill some practical wisdom out of the experience of the managers with whom it has been my privilege to work. Some of these experiences turned out successfully and others did not; but in every case there is a lesson to be learned. My own role has simply been to recount what happened and to try to distill the lessons.

To oversimplify a bit, one can distinguish three kinds of managers:

—Those who learn little or nothing from their own experience and continue managing today with few, if any, more insights into what they are doing than they possessed when they began to direct the work of others. This book will be of little value to them.

—Those who continually analyze their own experience in hopes of deriving some principles which can guide them toward greater effectiveness. To the extent that this book relates to their own experience, they may find it helpful.

—Those who supplement their own experience with that of others, in hopes of learning quickly what equally clever managers may have taken months or years to learn for themselves. The laws of chance heavily favor this kind of manager, and this book may be quite helpful to them.

This book is written chiefly for practicing managers at the middle or lower levels and for persons (including students) who may embark upon managerial careers. It is designed to improve their effectiveness in managing other people's work, and for that reason it is almost entirely concerned with the ways in which managers and subordinates affect each other directly. It ventures into their relationships with each other and with the larger organization of which they are a part (for example, with personnel departments and policies) only to the extent needed to clarify the context in which manager-subordinate relationships are worked out.

The underlying convictions on which this book is based are:

—that most managers can learn to manage their subordinates more effectively than they do

—that effectiveness in managing subordinates makes a significant economic difference for the organization
—that lower-level managers in general (and first-level supervisors in particular) are crucially important to any organization's ultimate success

—that the best interests of subordinates are served when their organizational superiors have a professional commitment to their own managerial effectiveness

The reader will find no footnotes or bibliographic references. The case material is drawn entirely from my own consulting experience. Although the book is designed as much for students as for practicing managers, I have deliberately made it as untheoretical as possible and have tried instead to stress the inelegant realities that both of them will encounter sooner or later. Nevertheless, the methods presented here and the conclusions drawn from them are at least broadly consistent with the mainstream of current thinking in the applied behavioral sciences.

Certain sections of the book have appeared elsewhere. Part of Chapter 3 appeared in the March-April 1976 issue of the *Harvard Business Review*. Parts of Chapter 7 appeared in the July 1973 issue of the *Conference Board Record*, and part of Chapter 8 appeared in the March 1974 issue of the same publication. Another part of Chapter 8 appeared in the "Leader's Guide" for my film series, *Effective Supervision*, produced by BNA Communications, Inc., in 1974. The permission of the editors to use this material is gratefully acknowledged.

S.W.G.

Ho-Ho-Kus, New Jersey
March 1976

Contents

Saul W. Gellerman
Managers and Subordinates

Chapter 1
Individuals and Organizations

The bulk of the world's work is done by organizations, rather than by individuals like you and me. But organizations are made up of individuals, and in the relationship between them there is an inescapable paradox. Briefly, while organizations are totally dependent on individual effort, they are compelled to risk suppressing it or diverting it into unproductive channels. There is a very wide variation in the effectiveness with which organizations manage the paradox, and this accounts in no small way for the variation in the economic results that they achieve.

The economic justification for any organization's existence is its ability to accomplish more than the sum of what its members could accomplish if they acted alone. A properly functioning organization *multiplies* the capacity of its members to achieve useful ends—partly by providing them with technical means and information they could seldom provide for themselves, but mostly by influencing their behavior so that they act in a prescribed, coordinated way. It is this latter function of management—the behavioral aspect—with which we are primarily concerned.

Like everything else in life, membership in an organization involves a trade-off between benefits and costs, in this case between the economic and other advantages of membership and the loss—to one degree or another—of personal freedom. For the simple fact is that organizations cannot function if all (or even a significant minority) of its members are doing whatever they please instead of whatever the organization requires of them. Therefore organizations find it necessary to require members to act in ways they might not act if they were not members.

The risk of untoward reactions comes not so much from the particular things an organization expects its members to do as from the *requirement* that they do them. The organization has little choice but to insist, and to employ whatever sanctions it has to make its insistence stick, since its economic health and perhaps survival may be at stake. But to be given no choice in the governance of one's own behavior, no matter how logical the reasons for it, is a distasteful experience for most people—and worse than that for many. Obviously, most people have been willing to make the trade-off; otherwise organizations could not have flourished to the extent they have.

But a closer examination of employee behavior reveals that individual freedom is *not* simply sold for a wage, or for security or status. *It is preserved.* In many ways—some subtle, some blatant, but all of them meaningful to the individual employee—the score is kept even. The organization is made to pay for every behavioral concession it exacts from its members, not simply with a wage but with a loss of productivity as well. Thus the paradox of the organization's relationship to its members is that it can never escape the twin risks of failing to coordinate their efforts and of motivating them to retaliate—and either way losing productivity, which is the ultimate justification for its existence.

The task of management is to somehow steer a course between these risks. This is difficult but not impossible. Part of the difficulty lies in the traditional approaches to the management of subordinates which we have inherited from the past. These are increasingly inappropriate for contemporary use. But force of habit is one of the most powerful behavior-shaping forces, and for this reason it would not be surprising if traditional but counterproductive methods continue to be practiced for quite some time.

The collective behavior of an organization's members exerts a substantial leverage on the economic results the organization can attain. More precisely, it determines the efficiency with which the organization can use its capital; and therefore it also affects its profitability, its competitiveness, and ultimately its survival. Sometimes the principal reason why an organization is not destroyed by the unproductive behavior of its members is that competing organizations fare just as badly.

The causes of individual behavior are extremely complex, and collective behavior is even more difficult to explain in detail. Hence we are compelled to generalize. But generalizations become easier to express and to understand the more they depart from the facts, and the reader should be wary of confusing convenient approximations with reality. Generalizations can illuminate the landscape we must traverse, but they do not point out which path to follow.

Here, then, are some generalizations about the relationship between the ways in which people are managed and their probable collective reactions to that experience. These can serve as first approximations; later we will complicate them a bit and thereby bring them slightly closer to reality. With respect to its effect on productivity, employee behavior can be classified as slightly positive or negative, or highly positive or negative.

Slightly negative behavior is perhaps the most commonly encountered type. It includes such actions as deliberate absenteeism, voluntary turnover, informal conspiracies to limit production, and a tendency to take advantage of whatever opportunities for nonwork, or for mild violations of rules, that supervisory laxity provides.

That such actions have negative effects is obvious; that their cumulative impact is classified as "slight" may come as a surprise. But it is precisely such petty forms of resistance that high-speed production equipment is designed to overwhelm and that management control systems are designed to limit. To varying degrees, both may succeed. Further, these obstructions have been occurring for so long that management has tended to accept them as inevitable—like the weather—and to make allowances for them. Their costs are built in to normal overhead and are seldom questioned.

Slightly negative behavior tends to be a response to managerial pressures, attempts to create or to play upon fears (especially of unemployment), or apparent favoritism. It can also result from clumsy supervision or from inadequate communication. In brief, it is a mild form of retaliation by people who feel, rightly or wrongly, that they have been mildly wronged.

Slightly positive behavior is perhaps the next most frequent type. In addition to the comparative absence of the above resistances, it is characterized by a relaxed, informal relationship between superiors and subordinates and by passive cooperation. That is, subordinates do what they are asked to do willingly enough but are unlikely to seek opportunities for activity or to take the risk of initiative if they should encounter them.

The principal advantages of such relationships, from a productivity point of view, is that they are relieved of the obstructive burdens created in the "slightly negative" forms of behavior. This can be important when a change has to be introduced or when an extraordinary effort is required—for example, overtime to cope with a large volume of orders. Basically, however, the limit on the productivity of such organizations will be drawn by the abilities and motivation of the supervisors. Their subordinates will generally do whatever they are asked to do but will make no particular contributions of their own.

Slightly positive behavior results from managerial courtesy and thoughtfulness, from willingness to react flexibly to reasonable requests for minor deviations from rules, and from conscious efforts to be fair. In brief, slightly positive behavior is the reward of managerial decency.

Highly negative behavior not only limits the current productivity of an organization but damages its productive capacity as well. It consists of long strikes (as distinct from short ones, which are usually little more than bargaining tactics), sabotage of plant or products, theft, and boycotts. Such actions can reduce market shares and increase the cost of financing, thus continuing to handicap the enterprise long after the event itself has passed.

Such behavior tends to result from old grievances that have been denied or ignored—it is the denial or the ignoring, not the grievance, that produces the reaction—or from a desire to retaliate against real or fancied coercion. It is best understood as a way of settling old scores, and it may have had its origins quite some time before the reaction itself began to develop.

Highly positive behavior is the attempt by most members of an organization to put its resources to the most productive use at all times. It is characterized by active searches for advantages and opportunities for the organization, clever and sometimes creative solutions to problems created by everyday contingencies, a high degree of self-management, and willingness to take calculated risks. In effect, all employees treat their part of the enterprise as if they were its fully accountable general managers.

Although the motivation level in such groups is about as high as could realistically be expected, the groups are not managerial utopias by any means. Control and coordination are difficult to achieve, and daily operations may be beset by a certain unpredictability that some managers find unsettling. Nevertheless, on balance, these are the organizations which will tend to make the most with the least, to seize opportunities that others may still be pondering, and to react to adversity with a counterattack instead of a headlong retreat.

Such behavior tends to develop in open groups in which managers share their knowledge and present problems for discussion —not prescribed solutions for compliance—to their subordinates. It results from jobs that are deliberately kept loosely defined, so that responsibilities can be molded to the talents of individuals and expanded as those talents expand. It results from the kind of leadership that supports, rather than monopolizes, initiative.

Nothing in real life breaks down so neatly into simple groups, and organizational behavior is no exception. To make these convenient approximations fit better into reality, we must add some complications: a *time dimension*, the *effect of conformity*, and *supervisory skill*.

No sequence of cause and effect in adult behavior begins when that behavior first interests us. This is because no adults react solely to their most recent experience. They react instead to the totality of their related experiences, or at least to their remembered experiences (including those remembered only dimly). A change in a long pattern of experience will begin to alter attitudes (and subsequently behavior) only if the change persists long enough to eventually constitute a sizable fraction of total remembered experience.

At any given moment, a group is managed more by what it remembers from its past than by what it experiences in the present, simply because the present is never a large part of the total experience of adults. Thus a new manager taking over a group finds that in a real sense the predecessor is still in charge and will remain so for some time. Subordinates will be slow to react to differences between the two managers until they are convinced that the differences are real.

The larger and older the group, the slower its recognition of, and adaptation to, a changed management style. Therefore, merely to alter a management style in hopes of a more positive behavioral response is no guarantee at all that one will occur in the foreseeable future. There are no magic managerial formulas that produce quick behavioral results. (If there were, we would have no need of good managers; anyone with a good memory and little imagination would do.) Thus the manager who undertakes to alter group behavior for the sake of productivity may have to do it on faith, since persistence is essential and rewards, in the short term at least, are unlikely. Such an undertaking is therefore best put in the hands of a manager who considers it more important to bring out the best than to suppress the worst in subordinates, regardless of whether a tangible payoff is immediately forthcoming.

The effect of *conformity* ranks with that of past experience in the hierarchy of behavior-influencing agents. Its power is awesome. Most people have views of their own about the major issues confronting them, but they are more likely to confide those views than to broadcast them; and they are least likely of all to want to confront the advocates of other views in public. There may, in other words, be a considerable disparity between beliefs (or what people *say* are their beliefs) and action, when action must be taken before the eyes of a large group.

Thus it may appear that a relative handful of aggressive, articulate leaders can bend a group to their will, at least as far as overt behavior is concerned. But the appearance is usually deceptive, and the effect probably occurs not because the group fears its leaders but because each member of the group fears the disapproval of the other members. The effect of conformity on group behavior is not a case of "follow the leader" but of follow the average. Therefore, the most effective leader in such groups is not one who tries to impose a view but one who articulates what most people feel other people are thinking.

Any group that has existed for a reasonably long while develops a consensus view on the issues facing it. While there may be some dissenters, most members subscribe to (or at least do not take public issue with) that consensus. The function of the consensus is to enable members to work together in reasonable harmony by giving them a shared body of beliefs. To know what the consensus view is, and at least casually to espouse it, is primarily a badge of membership and only secondarily an expression of one's own views.

To disrupt the consensus is dangerous because it might also disrupt working relationships. Therefore most members regard few, if any, points of disagreement between themselves and the general consensus as sufficiently important to be worth the risk of severing themselves from the approval of their workmates. This is why external appeals (for example, from management) to members of the group on the basis of specific issues may be unavailing in bringing about a behavior change. Individual members of the group may actually agree with management on specific issues, but their major concern is not issues but the approval of their workmates.

Conformity, then, is a second reason—along with the time dimension—why changes in management style are unlikely to bring any quick changes in employee behavior. Most employees will continue to act as they think other employees expect them to, even if their own views of management have changed. This will go on at least until their views are confirmed by discussions with other employees or until a gradual trend sets in toward a new behavior pattern that is more reciprocal to management's new pattern. (It is worth noting that the conformity effect is likely to be weaker in smaller groups or in groups that have existed for a relatively short while—which gives the manager of such groups a definite advantage.)

In this context, supervisory skill refers to how convincingly the day-to-day practice of management communicates the stated intentions of management toward the organization's members. It is common enough for managements to issue declarations of the kind of company they intend to be, full of fashionable phrases from the latest literature of behavioral science and—as far as they go—sincerely meant. It is more common still for managements to refrain from statements but to harbor the purest of sentiments and the noblest of intentions with regard to the rank and file. But statements, sentiments, and intentions do not determine how the rank and file perceive management. Their own daily experience with being managed does that.

Since lower-level managers in general and first-level supervisors in particular have the bulk of the daily contacts with employees, it is their behavior rather than the policy statements of higher management that produces the employees' perceptions of their company. Management may speak of participation, openness, and respect for the individual, and it even may decree that these be practiced; but if the lower ranks of management do not care or know how to practice them, the company will probably be perceived as authoritarian, closed, and despotic. For practical purposes, a company *is* what its employees *think* it is, and their ideas are far more influenced by what supervisors do than by what top executives say.

Hence the skill, style, and habits of supervisors—as well as those of their immediate superiors who guide and judge their work—have a heavy impact on employee behavior. Unfortunately, these managers are subject to forces that tend to drag many of them into exactly the kinds of behavior—over-control, under-communication, and implied coercion—that elicit negative employee reactions. Indeed, one measure of the professionalism of managers at lower levels is how well they resist these forces.

The most important of the pressures that push supervisors toward authoritarian tactics is the weight of their accountability.

By definition, supervisors have to answer for what other people do. It is a difficult fix to be in, and it is hardly surprising that many supervisors try to protect themselves by imposing and enforcing rules designed to make their subordinates' behavior more predictable. Unfortunately, this approach is too easily carried to excess, in which case it becomes counterproductive by generating, in addition to predictability, dependence on the supervisor and a tendency toward irresponsibility.

Another pressure is the desire to minimize confrontations which could arouse anger and lingering animosity on both sides. Supervisors tend to overlook, or "choose not to notice," inefficient practices and minor violations which have cumulative effects that significantly damage productivity. Typically, supervisors carry out plans rather than make them; hence they determine the extent to which, in actual practice, the potential productivity of their departments is reached. But supervisors are just as human as the people they supervise, and they have needs of their own which often take precedence over the responsibilities imposed by the organization. Thus they may be less concerned with productivity than with avoiding quarrels and preserving reasonably comfortable relationships. If employees hear of productivity through executive speeches and posters on bulletin boards but find their supervisors indifferent to the quality of their work or to the methods they use, they are likely to dismiss the talk of productivity as mere internal advertising and to conclude that their company is, in fact, lax and complacent.

Finally, supervisors are every bit as subject to conformity pressures as anyone else. It is difficult to supervise differently than the rest of one's colleagues, even if one's own supervisory methods are backed by conviction and the stated wishes of management. The behavior of individual supervisors is heavily influenced by the traditions that preceded them, the practices of their colleagues, and the emphases of their immediate superiors. Mediocrity at any of these points has a tendency to breed mediocrity throughout the system.

There also tends to be a consensus view among supervisors of what most employees are like, and supervisors are likely to treat their subordinates as if this consensus view were true of them. If they do not resist this consensus—if they do not insist on dealing with subordinates according to their own experience —the consensus may turn into a self-fulfilling prophecy. That is, people tend to react appropriately to the behavior they encounter in others, and their reactions are then interpreted by the others as vindications of the wisdom and necessity of their own behavior. For example, if someone suspects that you are lazy, he may press you for effort; and when you react to that pressure (naturally enough) with resistance, he may interpret your resistance as proof that the pressure was necessary.

The generalizations we have offered on the relationships between management styles, employee reactions, and economic results may seem, at first glance, to offer a facile recipe for productivity improvement. They do not. The current productivity of any organization is the result of evolution throughout its history. Its future productivity may bear the stamp of deliberate changes between now and then—but only if those changes persist, win over the bulk of lower-level managers, and are executed with a greater regard for professionalism than for ease and comfort. There is a payoff in deliberately seeking to create a more constructive relationship between organizations and the individuals who comprise them, and the proof of that is the superlative results achieved by a few distinguished organizations that have managed to do exactly that. But the payoff is neither easy nor certain, and the proof of that is the much larger number of organizations whose productivity is achieved in spite of, rather than because of, their members and whose productivity of capital is depressed or hobbled by the intransigence of human behavior.

But it is more than just difficulty that prevents so many organizations from capitalizing on the talents of their members. Shortsightedness, naiveté, and some genuine philosophical differences with the views expressed here are also involved. Taken together, they effectively prevent serious efforts to turn the employees of these organizations into income-producing assets, as opposed to a mere expense.

It is shortsighted, for example, to concentrate on the gross measurements of an organization's performance—such as profit or cost/effectiveness—without analyzing the components of those measurements in depth. Profits can be, and frequently are, inflated or depressed by factors over which the organization has no control (such as weather or the interest rate) or which are likely to be short-lived (such as competitive advantages or the demand for its products). Thus at any given period there may be no clear-cut connection between profits and the trend of employee behavior. On a longer-term basis, however, the quality of profits depends on the ability of an organization to prosper under adverse conditions and to strengthen its productive base under favorable conditions. It is in this context that highly positive behavior can be indispensably helpful and highly negative behavior can be catastrophically destructive.

It is also shortsighted to seek to circumvent the motivation problem by simply pacifying employees to avoid highly negative behavior and then relying on technology to overwhelm any behavioral effects on productivity. Strikes and other gross interferences with productive processes are merely the most obvious handicaps that behavior can place on production; they are not necessarily the most serious. Prolonged restriction of output where workers control their own work pace, or prolonged use of shortcuts and sloppy habits where they do not, can exact a cumulative toll that is more costly than a strike. Further, these effects are insidious, since ordinary cost accounting attributes them to where they are discovered (for example, to wasted raw material) rather than to where they are caused. And the costs of pacification themselves may be onerous, since they often amount to little more than bribery and merely increase the "manipulated" employees' appetite for more. (Indeed, in such cases one wonders exactly who is manipulating whom.)

No technology can be more productive than the efficiency with which it is actually used, and humans are quite capable (whether maliciously or inadvertently) of holding that efficiency down. Further, lost production time on sophisticated equipment is actually more costly than an equivalent loss on more primitive equipment, simply because the equipment itself costs more. In brief, technology offers no haven from behavioral effects; it merely makes them harder to detect. Pacification eliminates only the more obvious behavioral costs; it does not necessarily eliminate the worst, and it certainly does not eliminate them all. Neither does it introduce any behavioral advantages.

It is naive to deny that behavior matters very much—that the system works well enough as long as people do as they are told, and that they are usually timid or venal enough to do that. The point is that most systems can be made to work better, and this is their only protection when costs rise or sales volume drops. It is naive to settle for levels of productivity that can be achieved without active employee cooperation, since these may not always suffice, and changing the behavior takes too long to make this a viable strategy in an emergency. It is naive to blame negative behavior on forces beyond management's control (such as unions or changes in the work ethic), because the factors management can influence are at least equally potent. It is naive, finally, to rely on mere decency to motivate employees, since that only neutralizes behavior without enlisting it as an active, positive force. The golden rule is a necessary, but by itself insufficient, maxim for management; in addition to being decent, one must also be effective.

Nevertheless, an argument can be made against the behavioral approach to organizational management. That argument is basically philosophical rather than factual since it rests on inherently untestable assumptions. Therefore it can be debated endlessly without the possibility of proof one way or another. The viewpoint and assumptions against the behavioral approach differ from those on which the arguments of this chapter rest. In the present state of our knowledge, an appeal to facts would be unconvincing to advocates of either side, since the sheer volume of facts defies classification and since it is easy enough to produce cases supporting either view. The opposing argument is therefore presented here as a respectable point of view with which the author respectfully disagrees.

Briefly, the argument against attempting to influence employee behavior through managerial methods, and organizational results through employee behavior, is that both links are tenuous; that the effort in any case calls for scarce managerial skills whose availability cannot be relied upon; and that the advance of technology has largely nullified the significance of both positive and negative employee behavior. It is therefore more realistic (so the argument goes) to continue to rely upon the managerial skills we have already developed—especially in the application of technology, hard bargaining with employees or their unions, and firm managerial control—than to count on improbable breakthroughs in the art of influencing what other people do.

Maybe so. But this book rests on the assumptions that the links are subtle but not tenuous, and that the required managerial skills are neither scarce nor difficult to develop—and are, in any case, less important than managerial attitudes, which are difficult but not impossible to develop (otherwise, why write this book?). It is our view that technology has made the human role in productivity *more* important, rather than less so; but it has also made it harder to detect. Nothing in this book is inconsistent with the further application of technology or with hard, realistic bargaining. Management control cannot be abandoned, but in the interests of productivity it needs to be applied less mechanically and autocratically.

Thus we return to the dilemma that organizations have always faced, and always will, as long as they are comprised of individuals. The organization exists, thrives, and survives by harnessing the talents of individuals. Its eternal problem is to do so without hobbling those talents or turning them against itself. This perpetual balancing act is the responsibility of management, especially those members of management in the lower echelons whose influence upon employees is most direct. The following chapters were written for them and for those future managers who will one day inherit their responsibilities.

Chapter 2
Motivation

Management's concern with the quality of relations between individual managers and subordinates is part of a larger concern for effectively motivating its employees.

Although the process of human motivation has been thoroughly studied and is now well understood, at least by behavioral scientists, there is still a remarkable degree of misinformation and oversimplification on the subject among practicing managers. Briefly, "motivation" cannot be dealt with intelligently if it is conceived of as a personality characteristic which some people "have" and others "lack." It is best understood in terms of the environmental influences to which people react. A good thumbnail definition of motivation, for management purposes, is "any action or event that causes someone's behavior to change."

Four aspects of this definition are worth noting.

—First, it is not "official," and no claim is made that it is more scientifically "correct" than any of the other definitions in use.

—Second, it is an entirely objective definition, since its criterion is action that either does or does not occur. Thus there is no need to speculate on the thoughts, feelings, and other inherently subjective (and therefore indeterminable) reactions of the individuals in question.

—Third, it is a neutral definition, in that it does not specify whether the behavior is desirable or undesirable from any particular point of view. It can therefore be applied equally well to cooperation on the one hand or to stubborn resistance on the other.

—Fourth—and the principal reason for using this particular definition of motivation—it is a managerial definition, since a manager, by definition, is someone whose contribution to the organization is made through other people's efforts. Therefore it is essential that the manager learn to influence their behavior—to motivate.

In some circles it has been fashionable to suggest that when managers speak of "motivation," they are really making a thinly-veiled allusion to "manipulation." If we analyze this statement in depth, we can show that it results from a mixture of fuzzy thinking, misinformation, and a predisposition to see devils where there are none. *Manipulation* used in a pejorative sense presumably means that people are induced without their realizing it, or in any case against their will, to act in ways they would consider contrary to their own best interests. If that is what the word means, then the simple truth is that it cannot be done. This conclusion assumes only that the intended "victims" are reasonably intelligent and that brute coercion is out of the question.

There are *no* arcane, subtle, sly ways of getting people to act against their own best *total* interests, as they define them. There are, of course, difficult choices—plenty of them—in which we must sacrifice something good for the sake of something better. But that is not the result of sinister plots; it is simply what adult life is all about. In brief, there is no realistic basis for moral qualms about the study and use of motivation, since the only possible way to apply it is to adapt one's methods to people's inherent nature—to try providing them with more of what they inherently want and to help them avoid as much as possible what they inherently do not want.

In practice, nearly every organization follows its own version of a more or less traditional approach to motivation. The differences between organizations in this respect are nearly always differences of style, taste, or emphasis, rather than fundamental differences of kind. This traditional approach has evolved over a period of more than 150 years and consists of four major elements, each of which was an effective solution to a motivation problem faced by an earlier generation of managers. Because the solution in each case was successful at the time it was developed, it has tended to persist and to be regarded as inevitable. Much of our contemporary difficulty with motivation can be shown to arise from the fact that these solutions are, naturally enough, in a process of gradual obsolescence. But management has been slow to recognize this and to adapt the traditional methods to current needs or to develop new methods.

The four traditional motivators (or behavior-influencing mechanisms) are *pay, direction and control, job design,* and *benevolence.* Each has a different history, and each has lost differing degrees of effectiveness since it was first instituted. But they are practiced concurrently, as a package, nearly everywhere.

Pay

Pay as we know it today is a comparatively recent invention, dating back only 150 years or so to the dawn of the industrial revolution. Through most of history, people generally lived, toiled, and died without pay, at least in monetary form. For that matter, it is probably true that most adults alive in the world today are outside the money economy. In view of the pervasive emphasis given to money in our folklore and in press accounts of industrial disputes, it is somewhat surprising to note that all the fuss is about something that is peculiar to only one part of the world, and to only the last few moments of human history.

The use of money as a motivator developed as the solution to an unprecedented manpower problem during the early part of the nineteenth century. A technological development—the invention of the power-driven loom—was at the root of the problem. The economics of this device demanded more or less constant attention from mill hands for many hours each day. The problem was to persuade enough people to come work the looms in the huge new "mills" that had been put up to house them. It was not merely that work of this kind was unfamiliar; the long hours effectively precluded any other gainful activity. How could a man put in a full day at the mill and still have time to grow crops for his family to consume, or look after a herd of sheep, or work at any of the home crafts through which people provided themselves with everyday necessities of life?

If money seems like the obvious solution today, that is simply because we are accustomed to it. It was not an obvious answer then. Money had been used as a way of settling accounts (or "making change") between bartering merchants and as a convenient way for the wealthy to store their wealth; but most people never saw it and got along well enough without it. To recognize that money, dribbled out periodically in small amounts, would enable workers to purchase the means of their own survival and thereby motivate them to work, was a creative insight of no small magnitude. Some unknown managerial genius, probably a mill superintendent in the midlands of England, invented the wage; and it has been with us ever since.

The power of wages to motivate has always enjoyed an excellent reputation, and for the most part a well-deserved one. While it has always been patently untrue that "all" people would go to any exertion to increase their cash income, it was true for many years that nearly all people would do anything to prevent their source of income from being eliminated. The fear of losing one's job, and with it one's source of cash, has been an extremely effective motivator simply because money is indispensable for survival in a cash economy. For all practical purposes, money has been equivalent to survival in the industrialized countries for more than a century. It has thus been linked in those countries to the most fundamental and perhaps the most powerful of biologically-determined instincts. Small wonder that pay developed its formidable motivational reputation!

But it is now clear that the nearly universal ability of pay to motivate sacrifice, tolerance of undesirable circumstances, and years of unremitting toil is not inherent in either pay or human nature. Instead it was a peculiarity of the period of history through which the industrialized part of the world passed until about the beginning of the second half of the twentieth century. In brief, money motivates most powerfully when there isn't enough of it available to ensure either survival or a decent standard of living. Once purchasing power and assured income rise to levels in excess of that requirement—as they began to, for significant segments of the population, in the 1950s—the power of money to motivate undergoes drastic transformations. When there are people for whom money is no longer the indispensable link to survival, and who are instead more or less "affluent" consumers with the problem of which nonessentials to spend their money on, the significance of money shifts in two important ways.

—First, for most (but not all) such people, money loses a good deal of its power to compete against other needs. It must be stressed that in very few cases does money actually become unimportant; for most people it simply becomes less important. This means that other needs, which previously might have been sacrificed for the sake of preserving or enhancing income, now tend to take precedence over pay. Two examples are the need for leisure time and the need for meaningful work.

—Second, money changes from a relatively simple motivator to a very complex one. This is because survival has essentially the same meaning for everyone—the continuation of experience, opportunities, and responsibilities—but once survival seems assured, a whole host of needs, varying widely among individuals, tends to surface. Thus for one person newly raised to the ranks of the "affluent," money may mean security; for another it may mean an opportunity to invest and grow richer; and for still another it may mean independence. In brief, our ability to predict how any given individual or group will react to pay diminishes sharply as the pay rises above the subsistence level.

However, some generalizations are possible, at least in the broad statistical sense that admits of many individual exceptions. Once income rises above not only the "survival" level but the "decent standard of living" level as well, it tends to have two more or less predictable behavioral effects.

One effect of pay which seems to apply to all income levels is upon *membership*—the willingness of individuals to apply for and accept employment in a given company and to remain in the employ of that company. Membership reflects nothing less than a company's ability to equip itself with the talent that it needs to maintain its operations, and as such its importance could hardly be overstated. In effect, pay (and pay equivalents, such as so-called "fringe" benefits) is the principal instrument through which a company appeals to the local labor force and, in competition with other employers, selects those people whom it can afford to employ at a price they are willing to accept.

Thus, in economic terms, *pay is a price*; more specifically, it is the price of the availability of talent. Its motivational importance is primarily in terms of its effect of distributing people with differing temperaments, goals, and values among competing employments. Thus when employers speak of "motivation" and "pay" as if the two were interchangeable, the only *behavioral* consequences to which they refer are those of accepting offers of employment. This is of course a necessary, but by itself insufficient, condition for the productive use of talent. In other words, to equate motivation with pay is to look upon motivation in an impractically narrow way.

Obviously, we need to motivate people beyond merely accepting an employment offer. We also need to motivate them to work diligently, cooperatively, and correctly. It has been traditionally assumed that pay, if only it could be properly packaged, would somehow bring about this desired approach to work. Some people (for example, union leaders) have suggested that "packaging" pay correctly was simply a matter of paying it out in large enough doses; others have argued that guarantees of uninterrupted future income would do the job; and still others have favored tying pay to some measurement of performance. But in practice, pay does not follow so-called commonsense rules. With few exceptions, the only consistent positive effect of pay is that it motivates people to join, and remain in, a given company.

The exceptions are jobs in which individual effort is directly and entirely responsible for paid results, where the net pay increment as a result of such efforts is substantial relative to pay without such efforts, and where total pay is substantial. In large organizations where jobs are narrowly specialized, where most work is accomplished by groups, and where pay in the final analysis is determined by budgets and competitive pay practices, such conditions seldom exist. Thus the combination of incomes rising beyond a minimum level and the increasing tendency of work being accomplished in large organizations has effectively decreased the ability of pay to motivate much more than just membership.

However, we have noted that pay has two behavioral effects. Membership is the positive one, in the sense that it benefits the organization. It is also the broadest effect, influencing people at all income levels. The second effect is negative, from the standpoint of the organization, and it tends to be limited to people whose incomes have not risen far above the "decent standard of living" level (a large group) and, significantly, who tend to view their pay as being *unfair* (a group of fluctuating size).

Perhaps the most common of the diverse reactions to pay, once it exceeds minimum levels, is to regard it as a measure of fairness. Much more than a crude comparison of one person's pay with another's is involved. Although few people are introspective enough to verbalize the components of "fairness" as they conceive it, we can infer its elements from their behavior. Most people seem to want to be paid in such a way that the value of what they give to their employer is balanced by the value of what they receive. Fairness then consists of experiencing the same *ratio of values* (of what is given to what is received) that other people are believed to experience. Thus most people do not want to receive the same *pay* as others, but they do want to receive the same *price* (or ratio) as others for their work.

Interestingly, the behavioral effect of perceived fair pay is zero. When people receive what they want to receive, they are subjectively satisfied, but there is no objective, discernible effect on their behavior. Of course, they work at a certain level of effort and cooperation; but if they perceive their pay as fair, this level is entirely the result of whatever nonfinancial motivators are present. Perceived fairness neutralizes the motivating power of pay, leaving the field open to such factors as job interest, relations with peers or with superiors, and physical working conditions.

However, when pay is perceived as unfair—when the value of what is given seems to exceed the value of what is received, or when others seem to receive a better price for what they give—a distressing psychological condition is created. If the situation persists or becomes worse, new motivators—which hitherto may have been unimportant or quiescent—enter the picture. The individual may now begin to feel that he or she is being exploited and that dignity, pride, and self-respect are under attack. Sooner or later, if the situation is not relieved, the person will be motivated to take *some* action to get out of this predicament.

But the options are limited. Individuals may complain and request a pay increase or may simply quit and try their luck elsewhere. Neither is assuredly effective, and both require a certain courage, so these are not the preferred alternatives. A third alternative—"giving less" by reducing one's efforts—is by far the most common. Pay that is perceived as unfair is likely to motivate behavior which effectively decreases productivity.

Thus pay motivates membership for nearly everyone, motivates a decrease in productivity under certain circumstances, and beyond that doesn't motivate much of anything for anybody. Not a very impressive record for such a once-powerful motivator, but that (alas!) is what a century and a half can do.

Direction and Control

Two more traditional motivators, direction and control, are virtually inseparable. Therefore we will consider them together.

Direction means telling someone what to do, or what not to do. *Control* means making sure the person does as told. Both have evolved into elaborate sets of procedures designed to accomplish bureaucratically what the old-fashioned supervisor once did verbally.

Thus the function of direction now includes standard operating procedures, manuals and handbooks, and even "management by objectives." The function of control now includes performance evaluation, quality inspection, and work measurement. Basically, however, these are all methods designed to channel the employees' behavior into certain activities and away from others by establishing rules, or standards, and then trying to ensure that they are adhered to. To direct is to prescribe or proscribe certain kinds of behavior; to control is to measure results and to intervene when they are not satisfactory.

Direction and control worked well enough, in the sense that their results were more or less acceptable and their costs were usually tolerable, for more than a century. Their results were a certain uniformity and predictability of performance. Their costs were a tendency for employees to deliberately restrict output and to seek safe ways to retaliate for the loss of dignity implied in excessive direction or control, usually by injuring the product or service rather than by overt opposition. Yet the ratio of these costs and results remained acceptable to management for three reasons, the gradual disappearance of which has made the ratio increasingly *un*acceptable during the last decade or so.

—Direction and control were enormously buttressed by fears of job loss and by subsistence level incomes. As long as basic economic needs were unsatisfied, the need for dignity and self-direction was readily suppressed. Most workers tolerated being ordered about because they had no acceptable alternative.

—Until the advent of strong unions, restrictive work practices were usually subtle, furtive, and ingenious. Consequently, the scale on which they were practiced was limited. With unions in power, such practices became blatant, crude, and institutionalized. Some are the subject of written agreements; many more are simply matters of tradition which arbitrators are likely to support on the basis of "past practice." Thus the cost of such practices is greater now than in preunion days.

—Management uncritically accepted high costs and low productivity as inevitable and sought to improve productivity (if at all) by investment in equipment which displaced labor or by relocating operations to areas where prevailing wage rates were lower. In other words, the problem of labor productivity was treated as essentially insoluble; hence it is hardly surprising that management did not solve it and instead tried to avoid it. Only when behavioral research began making its inroads in the 1950s and afterward did management begin to suspect that its own practices—specifically, direction and control—might be causing or at least aggravating some of its productivity problems.

Direction and control pose far more delicate problems today than they did when workers were economically marginal and when unions were either nonexistent or ineffectual. The problems are not new; but until the yoke of economic dependence began to lift, they were effectively suppressed. What was once merely muttered and grumbled at is now out in the open. The major problem is that the psychological dynamics of subordinates and supervisors tend to put them into conflict with each other.

Subordinates are adults who live up to demanding adult roles in the nonwork aspects of their lives. They are parents, taxpayers, citizens, customers, and clients; they serve their communities, churches, voluntary organizations, and clubs. In other words, they direct and control their own lives to a much greater extent off the job than on it, and this contrast can become a very sore point if it is not dealt with tactfully—and it often isn't. In effect, organizations which place, or tolerate, extensive authority in the hands of supervisors over their subordinates are re-creating a parent-child relationship where it is not appropriate, wanted, or tolerable.

Precisely because the traditional role of the supervisor has been to act *in loco parentis* (in the place of the parent) relative to subordinates, the job has attracted disproportionate numbers of individuals who enjoy that role. For them, the power to give orders and (at least superficially) make them stick is too often regarded as a fringe benefit rather than as a managerial tool to be used with discretion. When such supervisors are limited in their exercise of power, either by unions or by managements that restrict them, they tend to abandon all attempts at discipline and to adopt a passive, laissez-faire attitude. In other words, they swing from an attitude that motivates resistance to one that tolerates failure to perform.

Obviously, workers who are jealous of their individuality and their ability to direct themselves, and supervisors who relish giving orders and exacting obedience, make an explosive combination. A very large proportion of grievances filed by unionized workers, and of complaints voiced by non-union workers, are related to the style or manner in which authority is exercised by supervisors. Unfortunately, a self-fulfilling prophecy is frequently set up; supervisors often are taught to expect worker resistance, and as a result they deal with workers in ways that elicit resistance.

The following observations are paraphrased from a 1972 audit report of a major automotive plant. This plant had been suffering for a long time from severe problems of inefficiency, personnel turnover, and poor labor relations. While the effects of those problems were worse at this plant than at similar plants (which is why the audit was made), the underlying causes were by no means atypical. Statements in quotes are verbatim.

—*How is a foreman selected?*
He applies through the personnel department. Once approved by his foreman, he meets the selection committee, consisting of line managers and members of the industrial relations department. He is usually approved if he conveys his conviction that the hourly employees get away with too much and that he is just the right person to keep them in line.

—*How is a foreman trained?*
He spends one week with the safety unit. This includes making rounds with the safety engineer, whose comments are something like, "You better step into these guys for safety violations, or else I'm going to get a piece of you when I evaluate your department." He spends three days with the industrial relations department, during which he

is told how unreasonable and dishonest the union is, and how he had "better screw them before they screw you." He spends two days with the accounting and timekeeping group, during which he is told, "If you don't stop those guys from cheating you on downtime, you will get your ass canned."

—*How is a foreman motivated?*
In the event he fails in any of his job responsibilities, he can expect to be severely criticized. However, if he does his job well, it is taken for granted on the principle that after all, this is what he is paid for.

Given this kind of selection, indoctrination, and motivational approach, it is hardly surprising if foremen and employees find themselves in a relationship of hostility and contempt. Each side views the other as the enemy, to whom no quarter is to be given and from whom none is expected. But precisely because an automotive plant requires the coordinated movement of many parts, it offers a myriad of opportunities for delays and subtle sabotage. The supervisor cannot be everywhere at once, and his subordinates delight in thwarting him whenever his back is turned. The cumulative cost of such combative relations has been horrendous.

Direction and control in *some* form are obviously necessary for reliable, coordinated performance. But they have become sources of frequent, severe, and costly conflict. The most effective solutions found so far are to upgrade the quality of supervision through better selection and training and to redesign the direction and control processes so they are used sparingly, selectively, and, above all, with a light touch.

Job Design

By the early part of the twentieth century, the traditional managerial approach to motivation based on pay, direction, and control was a century old and seemed to represent all the motivational expertise management would ever need. Then, a new stage of technological development presented management with yet another challenge. In coping with it, the third element in the traditional approach—job design—was created, and like the others it persists to this day. There is, however, one major difference between this method of influencing behavior and the others. While all are in various stages of obsolescence, the others have merely grown less potent while this one has become pernicious.

The challenge was an imbalance between the productive potential of technology, at the level it had then reached, and the productive potential of the labor force. Technology had reached a point where mass production had become feasible. Enough was known to permit a transition from low-volume craft production to high-volume production of complex products. However, this knowledge was confined to a relative handful of well-educated people. The labor force itself was largely illiterate or barely literate and in many cases unable to understand English. (This was the era, in the United States, of mass immigration from Europe.) The problem, essentially, was to devise a means of applying technical knowledge with the limited skills then available.

The problem was solved, and solved brilliantly, by evading altogether the barrier posed by low skill levels. The solution was to build jobs out of only those "lowest common denominator" skills that virtually anyone could be expected to possess.

The mechanism through which this was accomplished was the assembly line, which is essentially a means of dividing complex tasks into a large number of very small tasks. This proved to be a superb way of using the skills of a low-talent labor force with highly productive results. Indeed it succeeded so remarkably that its basic logic quickly spread from manufacturing, where it had been invented, into all other facets of organized work. That logic was the division of work into small, easily learned, indefinitely repeatable units.

Two later trends served to reinforce the division of work into units that neither required nor used much talent.

—First, as organizations began to grow larger, a job which had previously consisted of, say, five major responsibilities was divided into five new jobs, each specializing in what had been one-fifth of an old job. Thus in very large companies we commonly find people working full-time at responsibilities that engage the attention of workers in smaller companies only occasionally. Whether this in-depth penetration of narrow subjects results in better performance by the individual or the organization is debatable.

—Second, organizations also enlarged themselves by the addition of intermediate layers of management between the policy-making level and the policy-implementing levels. These "middle managers" were necessary to help control what would otherwise have been unwieldy organizations. However, their effect was often to deprive lower-level managers of much decision-making power, with the result that foremen tended to supervise inflexibly and to demand rote conformity of their subordinates.

The combined effect of the assembly-line approach to job design, work specialization, and decreased decision latitude at lower levels of the organization was that the experience of work became progressively duller and more stultifying. As in the case of pay, the problem was suppressed and tolerated as long as economic needs were overriding. Signs of discontent began to appear in the 1950s, spread rapidly in the 1960s, and were commonplace by the 1970s. The reason for this widespread dissatisfaction with work is not that the work had become any duller but rather that the labor force itself had begun to change significantly. The roots of this change were demographic, but the effects were demonstrable in both attitudes and behavior.

By far the most important change in the labor force was its educational level. By 1973, the median educational level of all employed Americans was in excess of twelve years. However, since younger workers were the primary beneficiaries of the general rise in educational standards, their average level of attainment was even higher. While it is debatable whether the number of years spent in classrooms increases people's ability level, it certainly affects their self-estimate and their expectation of privilege and deference from those in authority. As a result, during the past two decades management has found itself increasingly confronted by younger workers who do not automatically concede that someone in authority necessarily knows best what to do and who are much less tolerant of unchallenging work than their predecessors were.

Two other trends have reinforced this reluctance of younger workers to tolerate dull work. One is the rapid spread of mass communications, which has resulted not only in raising the levels of sophistication but also, more subtly, in decreasing the deference that younger workers once felt they owed to older, presumably better-informed superiors. The second trend is the progressive withdrawal of lower-skilled workers from jobs considered menial (for example, janitor), partly as a result of absorption into higher-status jobs and partly as a side-effect of unemployment insurance.

Together, these three trends (all in the context of much less stringent economic pressures than in previous decades) have had the effect of making the younger segment of the labor force much less willing to do the kinds of jobs which historically have been reserved for them—the "entry-level" jobs which consist primarily of carrying out someone else's orders. These trends have had at least two significant behavioral effects.

—Absenteeism and turnover rates among young workers in jobs of this type tend to be higher than for older workers in more satisfying jobs. In both cases, the behavior is essentially a form of escape from an unattractive job.

—Waste, low quality, and low efficiency are more likely to occur where workers are uninterested in their work or where attention is unlikely to be sustained at high enough levels.

Collectively, these reactions to dullness produce a significant drag on productivity. As management has recognized that the root of the problem is in the way work itself has been organized, it has responded with a variety of techniques, some effective and others not so effective. These include *job enrichment*, a generic name for any of several techniques designed to match the demands of the job more closely to the abilities of the individual; *participative management*, using various ways of involving workers in decisions affecting their work; and in some cases, attempts to *distract* workers from the basic problem of dull work with music, frequent rest periods, or more attractive facilities.

Inappropriate job design is by now recognized as a serious problem. In fact, it is likely to grow worse, because the labor force consists increasingly of younger and better-educated workers for whom traditional jobs are ill-designed. While attempts to cope with the problem have had some success, large-scale solutions are elusive. Perhaps the most important reason for this is that job design is itself part of a larger mosaic that includes traditional approaches to organization structure, engineering, and the technique of management itself.

Effective adaptations of job design to the needs of the emerging labor force are unlikely to occur, at least on a large scale, without major changes in the internal culture of organizations. Such changes are inherently slow and tend to lag behind the need for them. Thus we are likely to continue to see, for quite some time, an uneven pattern in which some organizations adapt themselves successfully to the need for challenging work, others experiment ineffectually, and still others try to fight or ignore the trend of history. Eventually, the economic advantages which accrue to companies that adapt successfully are likely to bring the laggards into line with the new realities. But when that will happen, no one can say.

Benevolence

The fourth element of the more or less universal approach to motivation is benevolence, defined here as an action deliberately undertaken to influence the attitudes or feelings of employees— in brief, attempts to make them happy. The emphasis on benevolence dates from about the mid-1930s; prior to that it was undertaken only sporadically, and largely for religious or moral rather than productivity-linked reasons. Two events in the early thirties combined to change benevolence from an occasional eccentricity to a commonplace managerial method. These were the Hawthorne studies and the passage in 1935 of the National Labor Relations Act.

The Hawthorne works of the Western Electric Company, located in Chicago, was the site of the first behavioral research study of modern times. It began, however, as a straightforward engineering study of the effects of differing levels of illumination on the productivity of workers who assembled telephone relays. To be quite sure that illumination was the only variable operating, the engineers set up a "mini-factory" isolated from the main area of the plant; and to keep supervision constant they provided it themselves. Production rates soared as they raised illumination; but—disconcertingly—it continued to rise when they reduced the light level. Puzzled, they called in a research group from the Harvard Business School. Their analysis indicated that the engineers had inadvertently introduced a strong motivator, which accounted for the productivity gain.

The workers in the experiment felt that they were a favored group because they had been singled out for special treatment. Under the mild supervision of the courteous engineers, they developed a strong feeling of group solidarity. Productivity rose as a by-product of the fundamental fact of the experiment, which was that for perhaps the first time in their lives these workers were enjoying their work.

The original interpretation of these findings was that happy workers are more productive than unhappy workers. It has long since become clear that this was an over-simplification and that the relationship between happiness (whatever that is) and productivity is quite complicated. (There *is* a relationship, but it operates in complex ways and is subject to many exceptions.) However, when the results of the Hawthorne experiment first became known in the early thirties, they caused a considerable stir among business executives. Here was what seemed like conclusive proof that by following religious and ethical precepts, one was also following sound business principles. For many managers, this was all the proof they needed. After all, nothing is so convincing as hard, scientific proof of what is already believed. For a substantial part of the business community, "human relations" in the sense of benevolence was launched then and there. It has been in orbit ever since.

Of course, there were many skeptics. Also, then as now, many managers did not read very much about developments in their profession; hence there was another large group that simply had never heard of Hawthorne. It remained for the National Labor Relations Act to convince both the skeptics and the know-nothings. This law guaranteed the right of workers who wished to form unions to do so, and it led to the rapid unionization of large segments of industry.

In effect, management during the early thirties was influenced by two powerful forces. One of them (Hawthorne) implied that happy workers were more productive than unhappy workers; the other (the NLRA) implied that unhappy workers were free to form unions with which management would then be legally obliged to bargain. Either way, the importance of trying to keep workers happy was given far more prominence than before. Management got the message, and deliberate efforts to stimulate and preserve positive attitudes have been part of nearly every organization's repertoire ever since.

These efforts have taken many forms. One of the earliest was company-sponsored athletic teams, which survive today primarily in the form of bowling leagues. Social activities and facilities, such as dances, dinners, picnics and outings, hobby clubs, and recreational areas, are common manifestations of management's desire to keep employees happy. Company newspapers and magazines, especially those that emphasize noncompany news such as bowling scores and social notes, attempt to satisfy essentially the same needs. But perhaps the most ubiquitous of management's efforts to keep employees happy has been supervisory training, or that part of it which consists largely of short courses in managerial etiquette.

The results of these various efforts to distract, entertain, please, or placate employees have been mixed at best. Many of them developed during depression days when any gesture of benevolence was deeply appreciated; today the same gestures may be interpreted as attempts at paternalism and are sometimes resented. In larger companies, benevolence takes the form of standards of decorum and courtesy which are expected of managers in their dealings with employees; the more formal activities such as parties and picnics have tended to wane.

There is little, if any, evidence that being nice to people, or providing them with enjoyable off-the-job experiences, has a significant or lasting effect on productivity. On the other hand, they don't hurt, either; and when used in conjunction with more effective measures (such as appropriate job design and equitable pay), they no doubt help to ease some of the inevitable everyday strains of working in an organization.

Summary

Virtually every organization practices one form or another of the standard motivational approach that has evolved over the last century and a half. The gradual obsolescence of each of the four major elements of this approach is increasingly recognized. Newer approaches which respond more effectively to contemporary needs have been developed, but with few exceptions these are not yet practiced on a large scale.

Consequently, for most managers the challenge of effective motivation consists not of participating in pioneering experiments but of trying to practice some old and well-established arts as effectively as they can. First-level supervisors, in particular, affect the way subordinates do their jobs by the way they do theirs. Effective supervision is a demanding and difficult task, but if its elements are properly understood, most supervisors are equal to it. The next chapter will review some recent behavioral analyses of the supervisor's job.

Chapter 3
Supervisors and Productivity

In practice, supervisors have little to do with such things as pay scales, job design, or benevolence—except, of course, in the sense of administering programs that have been established by higher levels of management. The primary contribution of supervisors to the motivation process is through the functions of direction and control. These functions offer wide scope for differing supervisory styles, which in turn tend to elicit differing (but somewhat predictable) employee reactions. The impact of the supervisor's behavior on that of subordinates, and therefore upon their productivity, can be quite substantial.

For example, at a large, semi-automated factory, approximately 3 percent of the raw materials are "lost" during the manufacturing process. Instead of being converted into salable products, these materials must be discarded because they have been ruined by incorrect processing. Management estimates that approximately two-thirds of the losses (2 percent of its raw material inventory) are attributable to employees taking short-cuts and ignoring certain routine inspections and adjustments. These sloppy habits have developed over a period of years because supervisors have been more concerned with technical matters than with employee habits. In other words, the supervisors' failure to intervene has implied tacit approval, or at least tolerance, of the incorrect procedures. At this factory, 2 percent of the raw material inventory runs into the tens of millions of dollars per year—a high price to pay for sloppy habits.

Supervisors' impact on employee behavior derives from both *what* they do and *how* they do it—in other words, from both the substance and the style of their actions. Ever since the Hawthorne study, behavioral researchers have emphasized style, on the assumption that this is how supervisors convey their estimate of a subordinate's ability and reliability and how the employee perceives that estimate and reacts to it. Thus study after study has shown that workers are more collaborative (hence more productive) under a supportive or "employee-centered" style of supervision than under a style that implies distrust or low regard. However, simple observation reveals that both substance and style of supervision affect employee performance, that the effects interact, and that neither can be ignored. At the risk of oversimplification it might be said that *what* the supervisor does to direct and control subordinates determines *what* they will do—and that *how* these responsibilities are carried out determines the style, emphasis, pace, and individual flourishes of their responses.

In 1973, at the request of a major food processing company, the author conducted a survey of supervisory practices in the packaging plant. This was done by following each of twelve supervisors wherever they went for an entire shift, noting their every action in a detailed "diary" and interviewing them in their rare free moments to determine the reasons for their actions. The following excerpts from that diary give some of the flavor of factory life under high production pressure. They also demonstrate that what the supervisor chooses to pay attention to determines in large measure how subordinates will do their jobs. The supervisor's "style" also has effects, but they are subtler.

At fifteen minutes before three in the afternoon, C is out on the packing floor, speaking to the supervisor of the preceding shift. They had an uneventful run and are leaving C in good shape; all machines are up and the ingredients are flowing smoothly. At three minutes before the hour there is brief chaos as the first shift streams off the floor and the second, including C's department, comes in from the corridors where they have just punched in.

C moves down the line, giving a quick visual check to each machine. He also pauses briefly to tell each worker how the department as a whole performed last night. "Good running last night," he says. "Five hundred thirty seven cases." Then he grins and thrusts out his hand for a quick congratulatory shake, and moves on. Note that C gave the department's totals, not the individual's. Anyone who wants to know his own record needs only to glance up at the meter above his machine.

Later, C told me it is his practice to announce the previous night's results at the beginning of each shift. He shakes hands, however, only when five hundred or more cases were produced. Below that figure, he is likely to say something like, "It wasn't too bad, but we can do better."

C patrols continually up and down the line. He is not waiting until trouble begins; instead he continually monitors the places where it can start, hoping to catch it early. He checks moisture levels in the ingredient trays and pressure levels in the feed lines. If the pneumatic feed system fails on him, as it has fairly often lately, he will have to bring someone in to hand-feed the premixed ingredients into the packers while the maintenance men try to correct the problem. The alternative would be to shut down a packer, which C is reluctant to do.

From time to time, C pauses briefly at the "scope," a video display unit that he can operate from a small console near his desk. This device keeps track of each machine's performance with regard to running time, rejects, weights, etc., on a minute-by-minute basis. With the scope, C can determine whether effects too subtle for the human eye have begun to develop, and he can make an educated guess as to their cause. Based on these readings, he orders the changing of a belt—sure enough, it was starting to wear—and the readjustment of a knife. He feels a certain awe toward the scope, but this does not deter him from using it. "That thing is kind of spooky," he confides. "But I wouldn't want to run these high-speed babies without it."

C is no conversationalist. His contacts are brief, almost laconic. But they are also easy, with a touch of banter. For example, he seems to have a standing joke with one operator—a lady who is considerably

older than he is. She "won't permit him" to inspect more than one
pack at a time; otherwise she threatens to "slap his hand." Naturally, he
pretends to grab at a second pack and she pretends to slap; then they
both giggle, and he says he was really only making sure that she was
still on the ball. While his other contacts are not as demonstrative, they
are equally light-hearted. C seems to know his people well, and his
manner serves to make his inspection of their work, which after all is a
control function, easier for them to tolerate.

If his contacts are brief, they are also frequent. C is constantly on the
move, and in this way he gets back to any given operator in the
line fairly quickly. They see a lot of him without ever having to endure
a concentrated dose of scrutiny. Occasionally he points something out to
them, or vice versa. Mostly he simply walks up, looks at the various
indicators and potential trouble spots, exchanges a few quick
pleasantries, and moves on. He is primarily interested in whether they
are following a standard checklist of correct operating procedures, and
since they all know this list as well as he does, they are following it well. I
think the sheer frequency of C's appearances, plus the fact that
he comes across as helpful rather than irritating, has the effect of
reinforcing the good habits. In a sense, therefore, C doesn't have much
to do because he handles the *preventive* aspect of his control responsibilities
quite well.

In fact, a good run can be rather boring—nothing but the hum of the
machines and the endless mechanical march of packages into the loading
trough. Breakdowns provide a little variety and excitement, and
operators understandably welcome them. C knows this danger well.
His "visits" provide the only social stimulation the machine operators
get, other than relief breaks and lunch—unless, of course, a machine
goes down, in which case a small army of mechanics, supervisors, and
even higher management arrive on the scene. C tries to turn his
visits into welcome, if brief, respites from the monotony. Hence his
encouragement of gentle ribbing and of harmless jokes at his
expense.

Just before C's scheduled coffee break, the pneumatic feed goes down.
The operator throws the emergency switch and stands to signal to C, but
he is already on his way. "O.K., you did the right thing," he says,
reassuring the somewhat uncertain operator. "Clean up what you can
and I'll get someone to hand-feed for you." He is off to the nearest
telephone to call in a maintenance crew to repair the feed line and
someone from the labor pool to do the hand-feeding. The supervisor from
the next department arrives; he is scheduled to "cover" both departments

during C's break. C waves him off. "No luck tonight," he laughs. "You drink an extra cup for me on your break." Then he heads back to the stricken machine.

Things start happening fast. A large tub is wheeled up, full of premixed ingredients. A young man arrives from the labor pool. C demonstrates patiently how to hand-feed the machine, using a small metal scoop. Then he instructs the operator to start up again and glances quickly at his watch, noting with quiet satisfaction that the machine was down for only four minutes. As he checks to make sure that the machine is operating correctly, the maintenance crew arrives. C tells the crew chief what happened and then returns to the hand-feeder, making sure he is properly timing his delivery of ingredients into the hopper. A word of caution before he leaves: "I know you'd rather watch what those maintenance boys are doing, but I want you to keep your eyes at this level-marker in the hopper."

The maintenance crew chief emerges from the bowels of the pneumatic feed system with bad news. It may take a couple of hours to fix. C takes it calmly. The hand-feeder will be disappointed, because that means at least two hours of drudgery, and the operator will be constantly looking over his shoulder at the hand-feeder because he doesn't trust him to keep his mind on his work. "Don't you worry, Lester," says C. "You just lost four minutes, that's all." Lester doesn't seem convinced, but C keeps on reassuring him through the next few hours.

I ask C for his opinion on why the pneumatic feed failed. He grins and says it was a preventable defect. "But when a supervisor is running good he doesn't want to shut down his line for preventive maintenance. It was just my turn to get caught tonight." I ask if this was because the shifts tend to compete with each other. "They're not supposed to, but they do," he replies. Everyone knows that sooner or later a piece of equipment will fail, but everyone keeps it running in hopes that it will fail on another shift.

Off at the far end a cleaning crew moves in to give one of the machines a routine swabbing out. The operator and his two helpers stand aside during this process, which takes about five or six minutes. "Watch that end machine," says C. The cleaning crew finishes its work, and as they prepare to leave, the operator and his helpers move right back in. They are back in operation almost before the cleaning crew leaves. "See that?" says C, with obvious pride. "They went right back into production without waiting to be told. Those are good people." I decide to probe C a bit, so I ask, "Did they do that for my benefit?" "Hell, no," replies C. "No way can you run five hundred cases with a lazy crew—not on this floor."

C is highly rated by his superiors. His department's productivity is among the highest in the factory. This is partly due to the fact that he has a high proportion of seasoned, mature subordinates. But in large measure it is the result of his approach to supervision. The *substance* of C's supervision is his frequent checking and repeated demonstration that he expects his people to follow correct procedures. C's style is a mixture of gentle humor and reassurance. His pride in his subordinates is genuine and not a device, but it serves to reinforce an already favorable relationship with them. Unhappily, C is not a typical supervisor, and his easy, positive relationship with his people is not easy to attain.

L is a supervisor on the night shift, from 11 p.m. to 7 a.m. This shift has certain built-in handicaps: a high proportion of relatively inexperienced workers, a relatively small force of maintenance men, and an almost universal desire by its employees to transfer to one of the other shifts. Thus the supervisory job on this shift is in some ways more demanding than on the other two.

At 10:55, L is out in the corridor near the time clock, watching his subordinates punch in. They remove their cards from the "out" rack, insert them into the time clock, and place them in the "in" rack. Promptly at 11:00, L pulls the remaining cards in the "out" rack—representing absentees or workers who will arrive late—and walks rapidly onto the production floor. Taking a whistle from his pocket, he blows hard to signal that production should now commence. Other supervisors are also blowing whistles in other areas, and for a while there is quite a din. L moves quickly down the line to make sure that the people who are present are at their proper stations. He then calls his superior to ask for replacements for the absentees—there are three people missing tonight.

L is very energetic. He moves around a lot, and in a physical sense he works hard. However, he is largely concerned with the availability of supplies and the condition of the equipment. His concern with subordinates is primarily with regard to *where* they are; if they are in the right place, that seems to satisfy him; and if they are not, he insists that they return. He does very little scrutinizing of their work.

By 11:20 the "absentees" have all shown up—all were late. They don't seem particularly sheepish about it, and L shows no reaction either, other than to mark their timecards and send their replacements back to the labor pool. Evidently lateness is a common occurrence on this shift. For the moment everything is going well, and L hangs back, watching from a distance, alert but not directly involved. There is a certain light camaraderie among the crews on the machines. A cleaning crew is sitting on stools near some pillars, not conspicuously busy. I mention this to L, and he replies that it's all right because we are running well and none of the machines has gotten too dirty. I wonder to myself how dirty is "too dirty" and whether the cleaners' role is prevention or repair.

Now and then a worker approaches L with some information or a request. He makes a point of addressing each worker by name, and afterwards he stresses to me the importance of knowing each employee's name. He also points to a high stool near his desk at one end of the line. The line is so long that the only way to see all of it at once would be to perch on the stool. But L tells me he sits there so seldom that his people are surprised when he does. He evidently equates sitting with not working. Am I imagining things, or is L making a special effort to impress me? He was told the truth—that I am studying the supervisory job, not individual supervisors—but evidently he is playing it safe, just in case we weren't being entirely candid!

As we walk along the line together, L points to an employee whose machine has jammed. The employee is reaching into the loading trough, pulling out and discarding the packages that are stuck there. L notes that this is an incorrect procedure which has, in fact, been the subject of a recent series of meetings between supervisors and operators. The practice is unsafe and inefficient. I ask L if he is going to stop the employee, and he says no, because the employee has very nearly cleared the jam already. Somewhat later, he returns to the subject and adds two more reaons for not taking action. First, the employee was trying to get production started again, and he didn't want to discourage that, even if the prescribed methods were not used. Second, the employee would only resent it if he was corrected, and would find some way to "get even," probably at the expense of productivity.

There are several breakdowns during this shift, and L spends a good deal of time at the site of each of them. He is obviously anxious to get the machines back into operation, but there isn't a great deal he can do, since the labor contract requires that only a union maintenance man can work on the machines. L tells me he has had grievances filed against him for such prohibited acts as tapping an out-of-line part with a hammer. Therefore he tends to hover in the background as the maintenance man works, sometimes offering suggestions which are not necessarily followed. The maintenance man does not report to L but to a maintenance supervisor, who covers the entire plant at night and who therefore shows up only infrequently.

L is greatly relieved when the machines are restored to production and immediately resumes patrolling his line. In almost every case he discovers trouble of one kind or another that had begun to develop while he was preoccupied with the breakdown. I ask him if it would not have been better to resume his patrols as soon as he knew the maintenance man was on the job, instead of remaining on the scene during the entire repair. He replies that the best way to make sure the machine is repaired as quickly as possible is to stay with the maintenance man, thus guaranteeing that he will not slow down or take it easy.

About ten minutes before the shift ends, L is scrambling down the line, reading production meters on each machine and recording the results on a card. The operators shut down their machines after he reads their meters and begin to clean up the area or, in some cases, to chat idly with each other or with the incoming employees from the next shift. Some line up at the time clock so as not to get caught in the rush when the shift officially ends and everyone wants to punch out at once. By the time L finishes reading the meters his department is completely inoperative, with about five minutes left to go. He stands at his desk, transferring the production figures from the card on which he has noted them down to his shift report. He notes with annoyance that a few of his employees are not standing by their machines but have drifted over to the time clocks. He says he has spoken to them about it but that they see no sense in standing by the machines after he has read their meters.

I ask L if he could not read their meters with one or two minutes left to go, since that is about all the time it seems to take. He replies that it would be too confusing with the next shift coming on, and besides, his workers need a chance to clean up. I could not help suspecting that L was rationalizing and that his real reason was that to follow my suggestion would delay his own departure from the plant by a few additional minutes. As it was he left the floor promptly when the bell rang, dropped off his shift report in his manager's office, and left directly for home. Operators can clean up their areas at any time without shutting down their machines, and the entry of the next shift would not be a serious obstacle to reading the meters. L's shift is scheduled to operate for 450 minutes—eight hours, minus a lunch break—so his way of ending the shift costs him somewhere between 1 percent and 2 percent of his potential production.

It is not surprising that L is not highly rated by management, and that his department's productivity record tends to be rather poor. In comparing him with C, the question inevitably arises as to whether the difference in their productivity results from their supervisory methods or from other factors, such as the maturity of their workers. This is more than just a theoretical problem, since combinations like these—an effective supervisor with a mature group, a less effective supervisor with a less effective group—are not unusual. Management frequently tries to concentrate its strength in certain areas so as to maximize productivity there and is willing to settle for less production elsewhere.

Undoubtedly, both factors—supervisory methods and employee qualifications—are involved. But the proof that supervisory methods play a significant role is that less effective supervisors than C, working on the same shift and with essentially the same level of experience among their workers, cannot match C's sustained productive output; and supervisors more skilled than L, also on the same shift and with the same caliber of employees, consistently outproduce his department.

The *substance* of L's supervision includes checking the location, but not the activity, of his subordinates, avoiding insistence on prescribed procedures, hovering around the site of a breakdown while risking loss of control of the rest of his line, and reading his meters earlier than necessary. His *style* includes the regular use of first names in all employee contacts (most of which he does not initiate), a tendency to stay on his feet rather than sit, and much energetic rushing about. L works harder than C in the sense of physical exertion, and at the end of the day he is no doubt more tired than C. But L is less effective because he isn't working hard at the things that matter most. He is diligent and conscientious about secondary matters and neglects what ought to be his top priorities.

I meet D in the supervisor's lounge at 6:45 a.m. On the way to his department he expounds his philosophy of managing a packaging department, which stresses the importance of getting off to a good start. "The first couple of hours pretty much set you up for the rest of the shift," he says. "You get a good start, everybody's feeling good about it, and that will carry you right to three o'clock. But you get a bad start, people start getting mad at the machines, and then they get mad at each other, and then you know nothing's going to go right. Then you're just going to have one of those days, and you'll be fighting it all the way."

I ask D what he does to ensure a good start. "First off, I talk with the supervisor from the shift before us, and I try to tell him where his people are leaving us in bad shape. Like not enough supplies on the floor, or dirty machines. Sometimes his maintenance people lock up parts in their drawers to be sure they have them when they need them, which means maybe we don't have them when we need them. That supervisor, he's pretty good about it when you tell him, but he gets so busy near the end of the shift, some things just get by him. And of course, when you tell him, it's twenty-four hours later. Yesterday he did pretty good by me, but I always have my fingers crossed when I come in."

We arrive at D's department, and sure enough, the first thing he does is talk to the preceding shift supervisor. The poor fellow looks worn out and says he has been having trouble with the machines and the pneumatic feeds. After he leaves, D says, "When they get a lot of mechanical trouble on the second or third shift, they leave most of it with us, because we have more maintenance people." "Well," he sighs, "this is going to be a little tough this morning."

He moves out quickly into the line, watching each machine in operation. Two or three are shut down because the operators on the preceding shift have told D's operators that they aren't running right. He asks them to start up anyway so he can judge for himself how bad they are and whether they can be run for a while at slower speeds or have to be shut down altogether. His overall purpose is to determine where to assign his maintenance people first, since there are too many problems to handle all at once. At first I assume that he will assign the maintenance crews to his most serious problems first, but, on the contrary, they go to the machines that can be fixed most quickly. Somewhat later he explains his strategy, "If two machines are down, one with a big problem and one with a little problem, and you fix the big problem first, you'll have two machines down as long as it takes to fix the big problem. If you fix the little problem first, you'll have one machine back in operation fast, and the second one will be ready only a little later than if you'd done it first."

As repairs begin, the operators whose machines are being fixed busy themselves with cleaning and bringing in supplies. Some of those who are operating are having difficulties which will simply have to wait until the maintenance crews can get to them. D spends much of his time with these operators, offering encouragement and helping in small ways, such as rolling a stack of containers a short distance to where it will be needed or picking up debris. One operator seems quite agitated, and D engages her in a fairly lengthy discussion, out of earshot. As I watch from a distance, another operator looks up at me, smiles a bit sadly, and says, "We're all running bad today, ain't we?" I try to be encouraging. "Don't worry, we'll get it fixed pretty soon," I say, knowing full well I haven't any clear notion of how long it will take. I guess he knows it too, because his only reply is another sad smile.

But I can see D's point about the psychological reaction to a bad startup. These people are facing the possibility of eight hours of unavailing effort to overcome problems they didn't create. Some are depressed, some are angry, some are grim. Certainly nobody seems nonchalant! D is concerned that some of his people may just give up and try to get lost in the rest rooms, and the others may just sit sullenly at their machines, paying no attention to the dials and indicators and ready to snarl at anyone who criticizes them.

D returns from his lengthy discussion, and I ask him what the trouble is. Evidently the operator does not get along with one of her helpers, and she has given D an earful of her troubles. "That's always just below the surface with her," says D. "Just takes a day like this, and it all boils over. I just had to hear her out, and then I jollied her along like I always do. She'll be all right for now." I ask why he doesn't transfer one of the two women and end the problem that way. "I could," he says, "but then I'd have to transfer anyone else who got sore at somebody, and there'd be no end to it."

Slowly D's department begins to pull out of its slump. By working on the more easily repaired machines first, the maintenance crews begin to restore some measure of productivity fairly quickly. Of course, recovery slows as they move on to more serious problems. But D finally has some momentum, and he wants to take advantage of it. "We're moving again," he announces cheerily to those workers whose machines are still limping along. "Look at old number eight over there! Just hang in there, we'll get to you too." No one is euphoric, but at least the gloom has started to lift. D continues to spend most of his time with the operators who need help, leaving those whose machines are repaired to their own devices and looking in on the maintenance crew only often enough to be sure that they are proceeding more or less according to his expectations.

By lunchtime he is running fairly well. "When we're running right," he says, "I just leave them alone." He is still very visible, moving about the floor, but with very little contact now. He speaks mainly when he is spoken to. He notes with satisfaction that some of his operators have begun to help each other in small ways, something they are not required to do. "We could go down again at any minute," he says. "But I've got a different job now. The first four hours, I was just trying to hold it together until we could get fixed up. Now I have to start checking all the little things to make sure we don't start sliding backwards." He is referring to the many routine checks and preventive inspections he makes to catch trouble, if possible, before it gets out of hand.

I ask him about his belief that a bad start means bad running for the entire shift. "We've pulled out of the worst part," he answers. "But don't forget, we don't have any chance at all of a good run because we lost too much production in those first few hours. You ought to be here some day when there's a real good run. That's when you'll see them all happy."

After lunch, D is already planning for the changeover to the incoming second shift, still almost three hours away. He is ordering in supplies and putting the maintenance crew onto elective or deferrable work, simply because all of the urgent tasks have been attended to. "I try to leave the second shift in good shape so they can get a good start," he says. I ask him about competition between shifts. "Oh, sure, we all want to be the best," he replies. "But the way to do that is to have the best run you can, not by making it hard for the other shift to have its run."

With about thirty minutes to go, he proves that he means it. One of his machines develops an intermittent malfunction. It would be possible to keep it running until the end of the shift, though at the cost of having to discard a higher-than-normal amount of substandard production. This would maximize D's own shift production but would progressively worsen the problem and leave the incoming shift with the necessity of shutting down a badly worn machine. The repair will take an hour, and D could rationalize that there is no point in shutting down since his own shift can't complete the repair anyway. He resists that temptation, shuts the machine down, and sets the maintenance crew to work on it. The incoming maintenance crew will relieve them and will face a partially-completed job instead of the entire problem. D briefs the incoming supervisor when he arrives and then sets about thanking his subordinates for a good day's work as he passes down the line reading their meters.

Like all other supervisors on his shift, D is vulnerable to heavy maintenance problems. Therefore, his actual production record seldom matches that of a smoother-running shift. On this occasion, however, he gave a virtuoso performance.

Perhaps the most important aspect of D's approach to supervision is that he has a conscious, articulated strategy which he is continually trying to implement. He has obviously thought hard about his job and has distilled his experience into a few simple principles that guide him. Basically, he wants to get a good start, and failing that to develop and hold forward momentum as quickly as possible. He believes in allowing the natural dynamics of a successful group to govern it. His main practical problem at all times is to help that group to be genuinely successful. At no time does he try to talk his way out of his problems, by telling his subordinates that the situation isn't as bad as it seems. Instead he stresses the positive measures he has taken, and will take, to end their frustration. From past experience, they know he will make good on those promises.

The *substance* of D's approach to supervision is his strategy of deferring the slower repairs so he can get back into production quickly and his concentration of attention where he is most vulnerable—among the operators whose partially malfunctioning machines have to be kept in operation until the maintenance crews can get to them. His *style* consists of reassuring the discouraged, jollying along the angry, and leaving pretty much alone those who need no help. In brief, he gives as much support as is needed, and only where it is needed.

Restructuring the Supervisor's Job

Partly as a result of the study from which these episodes were excerpted, management undertook to restructure the job of the supervisor. The aim was to raise employee productivity by modifying the way in which supervisors influenced their behavior. Both substance and style were involved, although the emphasis was clearly on substance. However, as with any deliberate attempt to change a culture (and the accumulated traditions of managing with certain emphases for many years is nothing less than a culture), the main difficulty was motivating the supervisors to accept the change. For this reason, a much slower and less direct approach was used than might otherwise have been appropriate.

A committee of supervisors—the brightest and best—was appointed to analyze the way the supervisory job was actually being done. They did this by interviewing all of their colleagues, following a format which called for identifying actions that could be taken under existing company rules and that would have a significant impact on productivity. The underlying strategies were: (a) to meld the collective wisdom and experience of all supervisors into a single, comprehensive approach, and (b) to build any changes around their own ideas, rather than those of their superiors. The committee sorted through the mass of data it had collected and then chose ten factors which had been mentioned most frequently. They presented this list to their colleagues for confirmation that these were indeed their best opportunities for influencing productivity. Some of the factors are peculiar to this company and industry. Some, however, are more general.

—The supervisors' reluctance to correct employees who had drifted into sloppy habits. There was a long list of rationalizations for this, ranging from "it isn't important enough to bother with" to "it wouldn't do any good." The probable real reason for this reluctance was that acting as someone else's conscience is an extraordinarily delicate and demanding role that many supervisors prefer to avoid if they can. The cumulative effects of this avoidance included a great deal of preventable downtime, increased waste of raw materials, and lower quality.

—The operators' tendency to continue running their machines regardless of the quality of the product being made. The employees blamed the supervisors for stressing quantity continually while stressing quality only sporadically. This complaint was at least partially justified. Employees also claimed that quality was the responsibility of the inspector or the supervisor, not the operator. A related excuse was that the operators had their hands full just running packages through the machine and could not be expected to worry about quality. The operators' concentration on quantity was more a matter of custom, however, than of any limitation of ability; and the custom was one that supervisors had tolerated and even indirectly encouraged. The result was excessive waste of raw materials, energy, and employee time. It costs just as much to produce what the inspector must reject as to produce what is acceptable.

—The supervisors' reluctance to use electronic control devices that can make measurements of which the human eye is incapable. The usual rationalizations were that the "scopes" were unreliable or that a really expert supervisor could get along without them. The probable underlying real reasons were a reluctance to depend on something they did not understand and a feeling that using the scopes somehow lowered their status from experts with a somewhat mystical intuitive "feel" to mere readers of video displays. The effects were preventable shutdowns of equipment and a higher-than-necessary level of wasted raw materials.

—The supervisors' tendency to take good work for granted and to speak to the employees chiefly when something was wrong. The rationalizations were that employees were paid to do good work, that no further recognition was necessary, and that excessive praise would be embarrassing for supervisors and subordinates alike. The probable real reason was anxiety generated by accountability for failures. This anxiety thrust the less confident supervisors into a defensive position of continual readiness to react to real or potential failures. Those supervisors for whom accountability was a less frightening experience were able to adopt a more preventive stance, which stressed building good habits as the best defense against the growth of bad ones. Unfortunately, the reactive stance was more common than the preventive one, with the result that employees who had been properly trained tended to drift, through lack of reinforcement, into precisely those sloppy habits that caused supervisors to lose control of the production process.

Armed with these distilled views of what their own colleagues had said was wrong about the way they supervised, the committee proceeded to write and (with professional help) produce a series of videotaped "lessons," each analyzing the effects of a current behavior pattern, exploring its causes, countering the rationalizations with which it was defended, and showing how to deal effectively with the problem. The tapes comprise a course through which all supervisors are periodically put. They are animated, articulate "job descriptions" of what the supervisors themselves acknowledge their jobs should be.

Substance and Style

Although it is possible to speak of substance and style as if they were separate, in real life they are inextricably intertwined. Thus there is a certain artificiality in debating which of the two is more important than the other. Perhaps the following generalizations come close to describing their comparative effects.

—When the substance of supervision consists of emphasis on preventing controllable losses—when the substance is relevant to productivity—and when the style of supervision makes that substance easy to tolerate or even to welcome, the effect of that supervision upon subordinate behavior is likely to lead to consistently high levels of productivity.

—When the substance of supervision is relevant, but the style involves minimal contact, the effect is likely to be negligent performance with many sloppy habits. Similarly, if the style is abrasive, the result is likely to be conformity to correct procedures only in the physical presence of the supervisor; at other times these procedures are likely to be deliberately flouted, more or less as a form of protest or "revenge." Thus productivity is likely to be inconsistent.

—When the substance of supervision is irrelevant and the style is tolerable or welcome, productivity is likely to be low. Attitudes, however, may be positive; and in this situation it is entirely too easy to arrive at the misdiagnosis that the workers are being "coddled" and that what they need is firmer supervision. A change of style cannot correct a problem that is caused by irrelevant substance, but it can cause a deterioration of attitudes that could easily lead to worsened productivity.

—When the substance is irrelevant and the style consists of minimal contact, the result is likely to be low productivity combined with employee indifference. This might manifest itself in absenteeism, turnover, and tendencies to miss schedules, fall short of production targets, and/or waste materials. When the substance is irrelevant and the style is abrasive, the symptoms are likely to be all those just mentioned plus sabotage, frequent work interruptions, intimidation of would-be cooperative workers, theft, and other violent or near-violent manifestations. Obviously, in either of these combinations, the operations are likely to be economically marginal at best.

From this analysis it follows that *both* substance and style are indispensable to effective supervision. As conventional wisdom has stressed, one must be able to get along with people; but one must also recognize what they have to do to contribute to productivity, make this clear to them (direction), continually ascertain that they are performing correctly (control), and do it all in a manner that preserves their dignity. This adds up to a very demanding role, and perhaps that is why the ranks of first-level supervisors have seldom been filled with consistently outstanding performers. By the same token, that is why the recruitment, training, and motivation of *effective* supervisors is the single best route to sustained high productivity.

Chapter 4
Communication

Communication, in the sense that we use the term here, is any system by which people obtain information that affects their behavior at work. It is therefore a type of "motivational" (behavior-influencing) process, although often it is neither deliberate nor, from the standpoint of the organization, positive. Indeed, so many organizational failures have been attributed to poor communication that it seems almost trite to stress its importance again. The problem is extraordinarily persistent and, given its complexity, is likely to continue indefinitely.

This is not to suggest that efforts to improve communication are futile, but rather that effective communication demands endless sensitivity. Thus, if we make some realistic allowances for human frailty, we can expect to have to cope with our share of unwelcome situations caused by faulty communication. The advantage of studying and analyzing communication is that we can minimize both the frequency and the seriousness of those situations—provided, of course, that we *consistently* apply what we have learned.

Nothing is more central to an organization's effectiveness than its ability to transmit accurate, relevant, understandable information among its members. All the advantages of organizations— economy of scale, financial and technical resources, diverse talents, and contacts—are of no practical value if the organization's members are unaware of what other members require of them, and why. Awareness enables them to put their resources, talents, and contacts to work in a concerted, responsive way. Thus the role of communication in an organization is roughly analogous to that of a nervous system in a living organism—it orchestrates what would otherwise be chaotic. Nevertheless, despite its overwhelming and acknowledged importance, the process of communication is frequently misunderstood and mismanaged.

That process consists of a great deal more than what supervisors say or what managements publish. It consists of meanings read into their actions, and into what they do *not* do or say. It consists of attempts to interpret mannerisms and choice of words. It consists of rumors, speculations, and even fantasies, as well as facts and official announcements. All this complexity flows from the presumably "obvious" fact that a message affects a minimum of two people—the sender, who seeks a certain effect on the receiver, and the receiver, who has other needs. This fact is not really obvious of course; otherwise it would not be overlooked as frequently as it is. In brief, it is entirely too easy for either or both parties to a communication to become so absorbed in their own needs that they cannot understand the other's.

Managements sometimes have a tendency to believe that the act of sending a message is sufficient to make it believed; or, if the message is ignored, they assume that the trouble lies merely in the lack of the necessary showmanship and editorial skill to make it convincing. For this reason, sizable sums are spent on presenting management's viewpoint to employees as attractively as possible. This effort seldom results in great changes of attitude on the part of employees. When employees do not accept such messages, it is usually because they do not believe that the message is an accurate statement of what management really believes. And this is because they find it hard to reconcile the statement with their own observations and preconceptions. Thus effective persuasion is more a matter of presenting a case that is believable and less a matter of artistry. For this reason, management will find it more effective to use formal communications for emphasizing past deeds than for promising future ones. The following case illustrates many of these points.

A textile mill was established in a small southern city. About one-third of its employees lived within the city limits, and the remainder were drawn from the rural hinterland. Some five years after the mill was founded, a labor union succeeded in organizing the employees on its first attempt. The main issue in the campaign was arbitrary management decisions on shift assignments and promotions. During the negotiations for the first contract, a combination of inexperience on the part of the elected negotiating committee and comparative lack of interest by the union's business agent resulted in relatively few economic benefits. As a result, during the three years covered by this contract, the wage differential between this mill and other mills in the area grew steadily more disadvantageous.

A majority of union members took the view that they had been duped by a sly and sophisticated management. A minority blamed the union for promising much and delivering little. These views gradually divided the union into two factions. Then, about halfway into the three-year period of the contract, a nationwide recession began. Some of the other mills in the area were closed, and others had well-publicized layoffs. Union members were chagrined by the prospect of having to bargain for their next contract—in which they had hoped to make up for their previous "mistakes"—in an economic environment where management would not be dismayed by the threat of a strike.

Management then began demanding higher productivity levels, complaining that this mill, with its modern equipment, turned out less material than more antiquated mills in other parts of the country. The rate of production rose only marginally, so management began scheduling work on Saturdays, and occasionally even on Sundays, claiming that this was necessary to make up for the mill's inefficiency during the normal work week. Although overtime was paid at the rate of time-and-a-half and Sunday pay was double-time, weekend absenteeism was extremely high and the resulting increment to production was both low and costly. The main reason for the absenteeism was that those employees who lived in rural areas treasured their free time for fishing, hunting, and farming. They were reluctant to surrender their weekends even to fatten their pay envelopes. Besides, they regarded their pay as low to start with, due to their unsatisfactory contract. And, more importantly, they did not believe that management *really* needed the extra production.

Knowing that the country as a whole was in a recession, and that other mills in the same industry were shutting down or laying off workers, they found it incongruous that their own company was demanding increased production. In attempting to explain this phenomenon, they related it to their dissatisfaction with their contract and their desire to improve it during the next negotiations. Their conclusion was that the same clever management that had fooled them into accepting a weak contract was seeking to deceive them again. This time they felt that management was attempting to build a large inventory of material produced at a low wage rate, which would enable the company to profitably satisfy a depressed market for quite some time and, therefore, to resist union demands and even endure a strike longer than the workers could.

Convinced of this nefarious plot, the workers began various subtle forms of slowing production. Weekend absenteeism was higher than ever, and those workers who did come in on weekends tended to take Mondays off. Employees who had working wives or other sources of income, such as farms or "moonlight" jobs, began to calculate how long they could hold out if a strike had to be called.

Management, however, was guilty of nothing more nefarious than an inept communications job. What had happened was that just prior to the recession, a newly-appointed marketing manager had staged a brilliant series of moves which (largely at the expense of competitors) substantially increased the number of customers for the company's products. Although the recession decreased the average size of each order, the larger customer base actually increased total orders. Far from stockpiling material, the company was having great difficulty meeting the market's demand. Further, unless production could be increased, economic recovery would leave it hopelessly backlogged and unable to meet delivery schedules. Competitors, smarting from their losses and able to deliver more quickly, would undoubtedly swarm in and try to cancel out the company's brief advantage. Thus the need for greater production was genuine, and both the company and its employees stood to lose a great deal if it could not be met.

The difficulty was caused by the fact that the mill workers had not been told the real reason for the company's insistence on more production. Further, given their mood, they were unlikely to have believed the reason even if it had been presented. Eventually, the union president was sent on a brief tour of the company's warehouses and of a few customers' warehouses to see the inventory situation himself. The company also acknowledged that if its newly-won market advantage could be preserved through higher production, this would be reflected in a more generous wage package in the new contract. Although these moves were belated, they did contribute to a gradual alleviation of at least the worst aspects of work restriction and excessive absenteeism.

In retrospect, it is clear that management mishandled communications and thereby contributed substantially to what eventually became a severe problem. Part of the reason was management's disappointment with the employees for having chosen to be represented by a union. This resulted in management withdrawing from its previous efforts to keep employees informed. The reaction is not uncommon after successful union organization drives, and it is comparable in some respects to the reaction of a spurned suitor, who, to minimize the pain of his disappointment, reduces the number and duration of his meetings with the lady who has turned him down. The difference between reality and the analogy is, however, critical. Management cannot seek a new love elsewhere; it must live with employees who have chosen a union.

When the employees somewhat foolishly failed to demand a better contract than they did, management took grim satisfaction from the knowledge that sooner or later the workers would realize that unionization had not brought them significant benefits. What management did not reckon with was that a majority of employees would blame management, not the union, for their predicament. When the marketing moves suddenly increased the company's production requirements, management presented the problem to the workers in terms of the deficiencies of their work rather than in terms of the opportunity created by the company's marketing success.

In brief, each side found itself frozen into an adversary relationship with the other side, which the other side did little or nothing to dispel. Each side was licking its wounds—management's disappointment in the fact of unionization and the union's disappointment in its contract—and each interpreted the other's moves in terms of its own need to avoid blame and get revenge for the wound. The fact that the formal communications were incomplete and inept did not help, but neither was it the basic cause of the problem. Until each side was able to look at the other in terms unrelated to its own pain, communication in any real sense was impossible.

Rumors

The speculations on which rumors are built are usually triggered by a significant event that is either not explained at all or not explained satisfactorily. The persistent, morale-sapping rumors that plague many organizations are usually little more than the employees' best guesses of how management perceives those events. Certainly no detailed or highly technical explanations are called for; periodic briefings to all employees on how management regards its major problems, and what it plans to do about them, could help to prevent needless fears and misinterpretations. Management's actions—even its inactions—are as much a form of communication as any formal statement. People read meaning into actions and are more convinced by actions than by words. To make statements that do not offer a satisfactory explanation of actions taken—or, worse still, that ignore such actions—is to place those statements in hopelessly unequal competition with rumors. The following case illustrates this.

A company that made accounting machines went through a transitional period lasting several years, during which the older, electromechanical equipment was gradually phased out and replaced by more modern electronic equipment. The company's strategy emphasized the importance of maintaining the revenue from the older machines (most of which were rented) as long as possible, in order to provide cash for the costly process of converting the factories to electronic production. One of the methods selected for this purpose was the assignment of extra service personnel to maintain the older machines in top condition, thus (hopefully) muting customer dissatisfaction with the necessarily slow delivery of the new machines.

Simultaneously, of course, a new service group had to be created to install and maintain the electronic machines. This group was composed almost entirely of newly-hired employees, many of whom had experience with other kinds of electronic devices. The new servicemen were given intensive training. Thus the company in effect created two service groups, one consisting of experienced employees who serviced the older machines and another consisting of less experienced (but, on average, better educated) employees who serviced the newer equipment.

Gradually, the older group developed the notion that they had become second-class citizens locked into a rapidly obsolescing technology; they believed that while the company was investing heavily in its newer employees to enable them to ride the wave of the future, the older employees were doomed to the same fate that blacksmiths had met. Morale plunged, and with it the quality of the service given to the older machines. The company was soon deluged with complaints from customers, who were convinced that the equipment itself was breaking down, not realizing that the fault was only in the maintenance. Some threatened to discontinue renting the machines, which would, of course, have choked the company's precious flow of cash.

The company's executives realized that the problem was with its servicemen's morale, not with the machines; but they misdiagnosed the cause, assuming that the low morale was due to the heavy workload. It never occurred to them that the men were actually upset by the apparent absence of a future, After all, the executives knew perfectly well that the older servicemen would, in fact, be trained to handle the new equipment as the older equipment was retired. Incredibly, the executives never had revealed the existence of this plan, and this proved to be a very costly oversight.

A series of "motivational" meetings were held with the older servicemen, in which they were exhorted to show that fine old spirit that had made the company great, to meet the challenge of heavy workloads with a positive attitude, to remember that the customers' best interests had always been placed ahead of purely personal interests, and other equally irrelevant bromides. Other than noting that the men sat stonily through the meetings and applauded somewhat unconvincingly at the end, management failed to discern that their presentations had only succeeded in answering a question that the servicemen had not asked. The result was an even greater drop in performance as the men became demoralized by management's unresponsiveness. Some felt that management must be incredibly dense not to realize what was really troubling them, while others nursed darker suspicions that management was deliberately trying to divert them from their real concerns.

Eventually, a small group of servicemen who were on the verge of

retirement took matters into their own hands and, in defiance of
company tradition, visited the corporate offices. They demanded—and
got—an audience with the vice-president. The problem was swiftly
resolved. Management recognized its error, and admitted it. The
retraining plans were amply publicized. Morale and performance were
restored. The threat to the company's precarious cash position vanished
like a bad dream.

This was a clear case of obliviousness to the informal communications channels. Management made the all too common
mistake of assuming that employees operated on the same assumptions that management did—and made no effort to verify
the matter. The lower levels of management, which were in day-
to-day contact with the servicemen and must have had some
inkling of what was really troubling them, either made no
attempt to convey this to higher levels or tried ineffectually to do
so. Management's appeal through the formal channel of motivational meetings was well executed, but it suffered from the fatal
flaw of irrelevance.

The lesson of this incident is that to communicate effectively
you must first know what is already believed by the people with
whom you wish to communicate, and you must also know the
reasons for their beliefs. Too often we are so absorbed in what we
want to communicate that we simply blunder into other people's
lives with messages that are irrelevant to their beliefs and needs.
Enthusiasm for our own message too often breeds a fatal insen-
sitivity to what the intended recipients of the message are trying
to tell us. Under these circumstances, effective communication
is impossible.

The Individual Level: Communications Media

The same contrast between the messages that organizations send
and what its members already believe is found when communication is viewed at the individual level. In this case, the contrast is
the more familiar one between speaking and listening. Even the
most eloquent speakers are likely to be ineffectual communicators
if they do not permit their audience to communicate back—to
provide "feedback." Would-be communicators must therefore

not only know how to say things but also be receptive to what the audience is trying to say. This receptivity is as much a matter of being in a position to listen as of being willing to listen. In other words, we find in communication between individuals the same contrast between substance and style that we found earlier in management. In this case, substance consists of the particular method of communication that is chosen, while style consists of both the expertness with which it is used and the communicator's sensitivity to feedback.

Communications style—in the sense of facility with words and sensitivity to feedback—varies enormously among individuals. To some extent, innate talents seem to be involved, as well as deep-seated personality factors that predispose some people to be loquacious and others taciturn. However, training and practice can improve anyone's facility in communicating, thus decreasing at least some of the variability in effectiveness among individuals.

But an even greater increase in effectiveness can be achieved by altering the substance than by trying to improve the style of communication. That is, the particular method of communicating that is chosen can be more important than the skill with which it is used. Before demonstrating this point, it is necessary to establish a benchmark against which to evaluate the effectiveness of communication. For our purposes, communication may be said to be "effective" when a message is:

received by its intended audience,
interpreted in essentially the same way by the recipients as by the senders,
remembered over reasonably extended periods of time, and
used when appropriate occasions arise.

All four of these elements are essential, and in the absence of any of them, communication is not effective. In other words, communication is effective only when it achieves some planned effect on behavior. All other attempts at communication, however artful or sincere, are simply so many words, so much noise, or so many pieces of paper.

It is also necessary to distinguish between effectiveness and *efficiency* in communication. Efficiency refers to the ratio between the resources (including time) that are expended in sending a message and the number of people to whom that message is sent. Obviously, there is no necessary relationship between effectiveness and efficiency. A message can be effective but not efficient; it can be efficient but not effective; it can be both or neither. Regrettably, however, in the greatest number of cases the communications *methods* that are the most effective are the least efficient, and those that are most efficient are least effective, with style having comparatively minor impact in both areas.

Far from being an abstruse theoretical point, this contrast between effectivenss and efficiency in communication has enormous practical consequences. A very large part of the blame for ineffective communication—with all the huge costs and inefficiencies it entails—falls on management's persistent efforts to communicate with the most people at the least cost. Alas, communication is one function where it does not pay to be efficient.

By far the most efficient way to communicate is through the written word. The printing press or the copying machine can provide an enormous number of copies of any written message at a rapidly decreasing cost per copy. These can then be distributed to equally enormous mailing lists at quite reasonable costs. Small wonder that this is the preferred communication medium of any large organization—and that most corporate in-baskets are jammed with documents that will not be read at all or will be given only a cursory glance. Reaching an in-basket is not the same thing as reaching someone's mind, but that is about as far as most written communications get.

Nearly as efficient is the mass meeting. We simply need a large enough hall, into which we can troop organization members by the dozens or hundreds, all to hear an identical message read to everyone at once. Thus in a comparatively brief period a very large number of people can get the same message. But as a practical matter we have to ask: Do they really hear it? To hear, they have to listen—and there's the rub.

By far the toughest, most intractable problem in communication is to get the attention of the audience—to make sure they are listening, or, in the case of written communication, reading. This is simply another way of saying that we all have our own mental agenda—the things we are thinking about at any given moment—and that others' attempts to "communicate" with us always require that we temporarily suspend our own agenda and concern ourselves with the communicators' agenda. If we persist in giving attention to our own interests rather than to the communicators'—a perfectly natural and easy thing for us to do—the communicators are in acute danger of communicating only with themselves.

How, then, to win the audience's attention and hold it long enough for a message to penetrate? Note that if this essential first step is not accomplished, the first criterion of communication effectiveness (receipt of the message) cannot be achieved; and consequently none of the other criteria can be achieved either.

The critical first step of gaining attention is complicated by the fact that certain signals have the effect of turning attention away. The method we use to communicate is itself a signal—or tends to be interpreted as a signal—of our estimate of the audience. Thus:

—A memorandum is often seen as a signal that the writer is not interested in whether the material is read; the memo is intended only to be filed—to prove, if it should ever be necessary, that the writer had expressed a particular viewpoint. Consequently, memos are probably the least-read form of written "communication."

—Form letters imply that the recipient is not important enough to receive individual treatment. They are seldom read with care or attention to detail, on the assumption that they do not apply closely to one's specific needs.

—The one-way lecture, in which the would-be "communicator" speaks at length but provides no opportunity for comments or questions by the audience, implies an assumption by the speaker that he or she has something of value to say to the audience but that the audience has nothing of value to offer in return. Life is full of one-way lectures, but a merciful providence has provided all of us with an adequate defense against them—we simply do not listen.

There are a number of ways to get the attention of an audience, but by far the best way is to admit its agenda to the discussion—that is, engage in a *two-way, face-to-face* dialogue. This is by far the most effective form of communication ever devised, and no conceivable technical innovation is likely to displace it. Dialogue is the only method of communication that copes with the stubborn, inconvenient, unavoidable humanness of an audience. It is also the least efficient, least convenient, most involving method of communication. In the paradox of the most effective form of communication being the least efficient is the explanation of why communication is so often mishandled and why it is likely to continue to be a serious problem as far into the future as we can see.

Due to the built-in peculiarities of the human organism with which we are trying to communicate, frequent face-to-face dialogue is the very best method for effective communication. No other method even approaches its efficacy. It is therefore an organization's best defense against communication failure and its best guarantee of orchestrating resources and talents toward desired ends. This is true regardless of how stylishly or unstylishly it is practiced. First we will examine why this is so, and later we will consider some practical consequences for organization structure and the design of supervisory jobs.

Frequent Face-to-Face Dialogue

For brevity's sake, the term *dialogue* henceforth will be understood to include the notion of frequency and the face-to-face aspect as well. These characteristics of dialogue are all designed to cope with the natural tendency of humans to give their primary attention to their own agenda and to be, to that extent, inattentive to the "communicator's" agenda.

The importance of *frequency* is simply that any message, however memorable, is likely to be retained for a relatively short time unless it is periodically reinforced. All experiences subsequent to the message tend to compete with it, and eventually the message is outnumbered, so to speak, by the weight of other claims on attention. This is why it is never sufficient to communicate a point once; even if it is received and understood, it is susceptible to being forgotten. Therefore, periodic reminders of all *essential* points (for example, safety precautions or emergency procedures) is necessary. The entire message need not be repeated; normally a summary will suffice. What matters more than the length of the repeated message is the length of the intervals between repetitions—which should be fairly short.

The superiority of face-to-face communication over more distant contact (for example, telephone conversations) derives partly from the fact that the physical presence of the communicator is in itself a message; it indicates that the person places enough importance on the communication to be willing to invest time in it. It also derives from the fact that a great deal of communication is nonverbal. Most of us know perfectly well that others do not always mean what they say and that words have nuances to them that we do not always share. We therefore need some way to determine what a communicator really means. Specifically, how sincere is the communicator? How much importance does the person place on what he or she says? Is he or she genuinely committed or merely carrying out some prescribed ritual?

Most of us seek clues to interpreting what someone says in that person's facial expression, posture, gestures, tone of voice, and timing. With the exception of the latter two, these clues are available only when we are face-to-face with the communicator. Granted that the clues are not indispensable; still, without them our uncertainty of whether we accurately understand the communicator is bound to increase; and the probability that we will not interpret the message in the way the communicator intended is also enhanced.

Dialogue derives its importance from two factors. First, any language is, in practice, a nonstandardized code. Many words have more than one dictionary meaning; but even more pertinent is the fact that very few people bother to consult a dictionary to be sure they are not inventing a meaning of their own. Thus words are never a completely reliable guide to meanings, and some means of standardizing must be found to enable two people whose private vocabularies probably differ to be sure they are actually discussing the same things.

The word *average* is used quite differently in practice (especially by managers) than its dictionary meanings. The word has a rigid mathematical definition and another perfectly respectable meaning as the central tendency of a distribution or the most typically expected instance in a group. But it has come to be a way of damning with faint praise, especially when evaluating people or their performance. Thus we hear of someone who has done a "merely" average job. (How can the most commonly expected level of performance be "mere"?) And when managers are asked to evaluate their subordinates for salary increases, the great majority are nearly always "above average," which is, of course, a mathematical absurdity. (If pressed, managers may rationalize their ratings by suggesting that the "below average" people who counterbalance their own "above average" subordinates will all be found in some other manager's department.) Clearly one is never quite sure what *average*—or many other words that have accretions of acquired meanings—really means.

The most practical way to cope with the problem of private meanings and nonstandard vocabularies is through paraphrasing. All participants in a dialogue can restate the others' messages in their own words or in terms of their own experience, and the others can either approve that interpretation or point out that it was not exactly what they had in mind. This method of "calibrating vocabularies" is, of course, feasible only in a dialogue.

However, a second factor contributes far more heavily to the superiority of dialogue as a medium of communication. As already noted, the most critical single problem in communication is to get the attention of the audience. Unless this is done successfully, the first criterion of effective communication (receipt of the message) cannot be attained; and, consequently, none of the others can be attained either. Further, formidable obstacles must be overcome.

—One obstacle to gaining attention is the natural tendency of people to give the greater share of their attention to their own agendas and only secondary attention to other people's agendas, including those of their organizational superiors.

—A second obstacle is the natural tendency of attention that has been detached from one's own agenda to drift back to it if the messages being transmitted are tedious, incomprehensible, or too long.

By far the most feasible method for coping with these obstacles is to invite the listener to actively participate in a dialogue rather than to be a passive observer at a lecture. The person's attention will quite naturally be maintained by active participation if only so he or she can time comments appropriately and phrase them to be responsive and relevant to the incoming messages. More likely, attention will be maintained by the individual's natural desire to maximize the chance of being correctly understood.

The superiority of dialogue continues beyond merely gaining and holding attention. Through the calibrating feature, it is the best assurance that common understanding will be attained. The "frequency" feature of face-to-face dialogue is the best assurance of recall over extended periods. The recipient's participation in determining the final shape of the meassge makes that message as much the creature of the recipient's consent as of the sender's intent and thereby increases the likelihood that the message will be the basis for the recipient's action in appropriate circumstances.

If dialogue is such a superior form of communication, why is it not used more widely? Part of the answer, of course, is that many people simply do not know it is superior. And not so simply, many people would rather not know, or not acknowledge, that "efficient" forms of communication (such as posted bulletins), "impersonal" forms of communication (such as memoranda), or ego-satisfying forms of communication (such as one-way lectures, which are satisfying only to the lecturer) are no match for dialogue. Briefly, many people would rather minimize their contacts or maximize their importance than communicate. Furthermore, dialogue is time-consuming and requires a certain amount of skill; and, above all else, it needs a new attitude toward the function of communication.

The most essential skill of dialogue is listening—knowing or being able to probe for what the other person is trying to say, in order to relate it sensibly to what you are trying to say. Listening is a skill, in the same sense that swimming is a skill; most people can learn, with practice, to do it well enough, even if only a few can ever become champions. And for the overwhelming majority of communication needs, we do not need champions on either side of the message. It is patently absurd to suggest that only a handful of communication virtuosos are capable of holding an effective dialogue.

The attitude change demanded by the effective use of dialogue is, alas, a much tougher problem. The clear implication of dialogue is that neither party is going to have it all one way and that the subordinate will not submit to acting as a mere extension of the supervisor's thinking. This implication does not really change anything; it simply describes a situation that has always existed. But it openly acknowledges that an illusion cherished by some supervisors—that their jobs give them a license to replace other people's agendas with their own—is only an illusion. Giving up illusions is never easy, but it is the indispensable ingredient of growth and a step that nearly anyone can take. After all, very few supervisors believe in Santa Claus.

Implications for Organization Structure

One implication from our discussion of the superiority of dialogue is in the area of organization structure. Spans of control—the number of subordinates reporting to any given supervisor—must not become too great to permit adequate frequency of face-to-face dialogue. Organizations are sometimes designed on the inappropriate basis of "economy of scale"; the more units that can be brought together under one grouping, the less expensive each unit becomes. The principle is valid with physical units such as machinery, but it very quickly becomes inappropriate when applied to people. Once the limits of frequent face-to-face dialogue are reached, a diseconomy of scale sets in, because adequate communication is no longer possible and the people who use the machinery cannot act in a cohesive manner.

In an auto parts manufacturing plant, one of the processes involved machines that were linked together to perform a sequence of related operations. A total of seven employees manned each machine combination (or "module"). The modules, in turn, were set next to each other and extended from one end of a large factory building to the other end. A total of thirteen modules could be placed in a single line. For years, the company's practice was to assign one supervisor per line. Thus each supervisor was responsible for the work of ninety-one subordinates.

Predictably, communications were poor, and there were many productivity problems. Management tended to stress the physical aspects of productivity, such as parts availability and the condition of the machinery, and to consider the primary problem with employees to be the enforcement of discipline. For the most part, the relationships between supervisors and employees were impersonal, due to limited contacts, frequent absenteeism, and high turnover. In effect, each supervisor found himself confronted with a rapidly changing crowd of rather indifferent strangers.

A newly-appointed factory manager began to ask why certain conditions existed and to focus on the unusually large spans of control. At first he got the usual answers. It had always been that way, it seemed to work all right, and it was more economical than hiring a lot of unnecessary supervisors. Presently it appeared that the most likely real reason was that the factory building was large enough to accommodate a line of thirteen modules. In other words, previous managements, by blindly following the principle of economy of scale, had inadvertently made the architect of the building the designer of their organization structure.

The factory manager ordered the appointment and training of additional supervisors. Then, in a grandiose gesture designed to dramatize his point, he called together his management team, took a can of paint and a brush, and painted a wide, gaudy line between the sixth and seventh modules. "That line is a wall, gentlemen," he said. "From now on, everything on one side of this wall belongs to one department, and everything on the other side belongs to another department."

Specialists in organization structure have debated the optimum span of control for many years. The debate continues, simply because there is no single answer. With too small a span (too few subordinates), there is a danger of oversupervision (depriving the subordinates of opportunity for initiative) and of an uneconomical use of expensive supervisory manpower. With too great a span (too many subordinates), the danger is inadequate communication, lack of identification with the product or process, and, consequently, low productivity and poor quality. To define the optimum point is difficult, however, because it depends partly on the nature of the work, partly on the skills of the supervisor, and partly on the maturity and stability of the work group.

When subordinates are close together, as in a factory, so that moving from one face-to-face dialogue to another is a matter of seconds, spans of control can be larger than when that movement requires hours or days—as would be the case with workers in the field, such as salesmen. Skilled supervisors can handle a larger number of dialogues than unskilled supervisors, and mature workers in groups that have developed some cohesiveness over time need fewer dialogues with their supervisors than less mature workers or workers in groups that have a lot of turnover.

At ninety-one subordinates per supervisor, the auto parts factory was far beyond the point where any conceivable combination of supervisory skill or worker maturity could have made for adequate communication. While the reduction in span of control was a step in the right direction, all it actually did was create one group with forty-two subordinates and another with forty-nine. In the context of high turnover, absenteeism, and one inexperienced supervisor out of two, even the reduced spans proved too high.

Only when the factory manager settled on one supervisor to three modules—a span of control of twenty-one employees per supervisor—did the communication and productivity problems begin to come under control. Interestingly, turnover and absenteeism also declined. While credit must be given to the individual supervisors, it is also clear that no degree of communication artistry (or style) would have sufficed to solve the problem. Not until the job was cut down to manageable proportions, so that face-to-face dialogues were possible on a sufficiently frequent schedule, did the supervisors' skills have a chance of being applied effectively.

Implications for Supervisory Job Design

If we accept these premises about a supervisor's job:

—that the primary responsibility is to maintain adequate two-way communication between the supervisor, as a representative of management, and the subordinates,

—that the best way to maintain effective communication is through frequent face-to-face dialogue, and

—that optimum spans of control will always involve some substantial number of subordinates,

then it follows that a supervisor must rearrange priorities so as to devote the largest single portion of time to contact with subordinates. Anything else—including contact with the person's own superiors, paper work, planning and organizing, arranging for materials flow, and checking the condition of equipment—is secondary, though certainly important.

In organizations where communications are poor, it is common for supervisors to say that they would spend more time with their subordinates if more time were available. They claim that they are unavoidably tied up with meetings, ordering materials, and "fire fighting" (reacting to the crisis of the moment). In companies where communications are adequate, it is equally common for supervisors to complain that they don't have enough time for paper work, planning, ordering materials, and so on. In both cases, ample facts can be marshaled to prove their points. Both groups of supervisors are under pressure to produce, and it is normal (and, up to a point, even helpful) for people under pressure to complain about it. Assuming that the complaints in both cases are normal tension-releasing mechanisms and have not deteriorated into excuses for evading responsibility, it appears that management has a choice between two types of supervisory complaint. If the ultimate criterion is productivity, it is clearly better to have the supervisors so engrossed in contacts with their subordinates that their paper work suffers.

Does it matter how the supervisor handles contacts, so long as they are frequent enough? Of course it does. Supervisors who don't really listen, but who simply wait until the employee finishes talking so they can deliver their own message, will be less effective than supervisors who listen, probe to be sure they understand, and then reply or promise to get an answer—and keep their promises. Supervisors who speak the truth in a harsh, demeaning tone will be less effective than supervisors who speak the same truth tactfully. But the least effective supervisors of all are those who cannot listen because they do not spend enough time with their subordinates in the first place or who do not speak the truth because they do not know what it is.

Skill in communicating is a valuable asset for any supervisor, and fear of not being capable of acquiring that skill has undesirable—and unnecessary—effects. It deters some people from accepting supervisory appointments. Even worse, it deflects people in supervisory jobs away from contacts and toward a preoccupation with paper, things, and their own supervisors. But for the great majority of such people adequate communication skills can be had by simply learning what to do and practicing it relentlessly.

Chapter 5
Promotion

Promotion is the process of advancing employees to more responsible positions. The advancements are not limited to managerial positions but include any assignment of more demanding work and/or freedom to operate with less supervision. In nearly all cases, promotion is accompanied by a pay increase.

For many people, an opportunity to deal with more challenging work, or to make one's own decisions rather than carry out someone else's, is inherently attractive. Indeed, the desire to "be one's own boss," at least within the limits that organizations can permit, is a healthy manifestation of emotional maturity. Thus opportunities for promotion frequently function as an important motivator. Their existence helps to explain why employees with otherwise strong credentials are willing to serve "apprenticeships" in jobs that are not really to their taste but that qualify them for more attractive jobs. Opportunity for promotion also helps explain why younger workers do not necessarily accept the job offer with the highest starting pay; they have their eye on the kind of work the entry-level job leads to and, of course, on ultimate pay levels too.

In many organizations it is traditional to regard promotion, especially to the first level of supervision, as a reward which— because it obviously cannot be given to everyone—should be distributed in such a way as to cause the least dissension. In such companies promotions are usually based solely on seniority. The underlying principle is that whoever has labored the longest under the rule of supervisors is most deserving of becoming a supervisor. Thus promotion is looked upon as a release from bondage. Unfortunately, this method of selection usually results in an excessive number of incapable supervisors—which is one reason why working under them tends to be regarded as a form of bondage. More importantly, selecting supervisors on the basis of seniority alone greatly increases the risk that the critically important functions of direction, control, and communication will not be handled effectively.

The awkward truth is that supervisory jobs are jobs, not rewards. They have too crucial an impact on the fortunes of the organization to be dealt with as rewards. They have special requirements of their own, for which some people are predictably better suited than others. The consequences of a poor choice in selecting a supervisor can be far more horrendous than an equally poor choice in selecting any of the subordinates—especially since management has traditionally been reluctant to correct such a mistake once it has been made.

Choosing supervisors on the basis of skill rather than seniority causes a great deal of contention. To some extent, this is the inevitable result of altering a tradition. But it is also due to a widespread failure to recognize that no two adjacent jobs in the organizational hierarchy are as fundamentally different as those of the first-level supervisor and the jobs of the people that person supervises. Supervised workers make their contribution through their own efforts, sometimes in cooperation with other workers. But supervisors can make their contribution only through the efforts of *others*. Thus the critical requirement for effective supervision is not knowledge of or skill in the jobs being supervised; it is the ability to motivate and communicate with people who have that knowledge and skill.

Partly because of widening recognition that it is foolish to use seniority as the sole criterion of promotion, and partly because promotion opportunities are inherently limited, many organizations have sought alternative forms of promotion that do not involve supervisory responsibilities. When these are effective, in the sense of satisfying important needs that would otherwise be frustrated, it is because the promotions meet either or both of two criteria:

—the employee is entrusted with more difficult or demanding responsibilities than before, and/or

—the employee makes certain decisions regarding his or her own work which were previously made by management.

If neither of these criteria is satisfied, then "promotion" consists of little more than a change of job title and a transparent excuse to give the individual a pay increase. This kind of promotion is analogous to the situation where students who have not satisfied the requirements of one grade are "promoted" to the next higher grade, largely to avoid embarrassment and to expedite their departure from the system.

Although the role of promotion as a motivator is clearly important, it plays an even more vital role as the principal determinant of the quality of an organization's supervision. While much can be done to develop existing talent, attempts to manufacture it have been relatively futile. It is unfortunately true that if you begin with a dolt and then give that person all the training, experience, counseling, and motivation you know how to give, the result will be a well-trained, thoroughly experienced, wisely counseled, and well-motivated dolt. We must therefore analyze the various ways in which promotion serves to fill the most critical positions in an organization.

Promotion from Within

The practice of seeking an organization's future leaders among the ranks of existing employees is a widespread, almost hallowed custom. Virtually every organization gives lip service to the concept, and a great many try conscientiously to apply it. The advantages to an organization of practicing promotion from within are:

—Employee morale tends to be lowered, at least temporarily, by the introduction of "outsiders" above the entry level. Hence the organization that adheres to a policy of promotion from within avoids this problem. By itself, such a policy will not cause consistently high morale; but taken together with other policies, it may help to produce an attitude of fellowship and a feeling of belonging on the part of most employees.

—Recruiting at the entry level is aided by the company's ability to point to individuals who have had successful careers since joining. This attracts both more and better applicants, enabling the company to skim the cream of the labor market from which it recruits.

—Turnover is no doubt deterred by the prospect that sooner or later one's chances of promotion will become very good and that in any case one need not worry about outside competition for advanced positions.

On the other hand, the policy also has its disadvantages, which must be weighed in the balance before an overall appraisal of its utility can be made.

—Promotion from within restricts the pool of promotable candidates to those individuals who were hired at an earlier time (usually for less demanding jobs than those they might be promoted to) and who have not yet left the organization. Any restriction on the number of candidates tends to decrease the likelihood of there being highly qualified candidates in the pool; and in this case, the combined effect of original selection for easier jobs plus losses through attrition tends to sharply decrease the supply of attractive candidates. The organization is often thrust into the position of having to make do with a person in a key position who is less capable than one who could be found on the outside.

—Recruiting above the entry level, should the organization ever need to use it, is likely to be handicapped by a fear on the part of candidates that they will be in unequal competition for future promotions with employees who began their careers in the company.

—Discipline tends to be lax (for example, unauthorized practices may be overlooked) when supervisors are asked to maintain control over friends of long standing. Although working relationships may be comfortable, procedures which depend on rigid adherence to prescribed rules are likely to be carried out unreliably.

—Uninterrupted relationships of long standing tend to produce a consensus of how work should and should not be done. Groups tend to cling to the familiar and to resist innovations. This can be extremely costly in periods of rapid technological change or economic stringency.

The trade-off that management faces with regard to promotion from within is between comfort and efficiency. It is therefore one of the most difficult of all choices, since, contrary to much popular mythology about allegedly tough-minded management, few, if any, managers are indifferent to disappointment or recriminations among their subordinates. Promotion from within, in addition to being blessed by tradition, has the enormous advantage of being easier than using the entire labor market as a talent pool. It has persisted for a long time for precisely these reasons and will undoubtedly continue to persist. While the use of outside sources to fill managerial jobs has become quite common, especially at higher levels, many organizations will continue to live with the handicaps brought by promotion from within or will try to find indirect ways of alleviating them.

Attempts at alleviation have tended to center on improvements in the way candidates are nominated for promotion and on their actual selection from among other nominees. Both processes are well worth a greater share of managerial attention than they have had in the past. However, it must be stressed that by tightening nomination and selection procedures, an organization is only assured of making the best possible use of the talent pool that results from its past hiring and subsequent attrition. Far from correcting any deficiencies in that talent pool, these processes serve only to reveal them. They are thus a means of using promotion from within more efficiently; but in no way do they correct the fundamental weakness of that system, which is the improbability of an adequate supply of promotable talent.

Nomination

Nomination is the process whereby managers recommend certain of their subordinates for promotion. It is unquestionably the most unsystematic and error-prone, but nevertheless most widely used, method of selecting people for promotion from within their organizations.

Nomination is encrusted with mythology. One old legend, so often punctured that its persistence can be attributed only to a deep-seated need to believe it, is that managers, because they are managers, are endowed with the ability to determine a non-manager's potential for management. The fact of the matter seems to be that the great majority of managers know as little about their subordinates' potential as anyone else does; that is, they know their own likes and dislikes and very little more. A somewhat more sophisticated version of the same myth is that because managers are in the best position to be aware of their subordinates' work, they are qualified to judge the implications of that work for promotion. The premise is correct in most cases, but the conclusion is a non sequitur. Simply having information at one's disposal is no guarantee that one will distinguish the relevant from the irrelevant.

As traditionally practiced, nomination suffers from four severe weaknesses, any one of which is capable of rendering it highly unreliable.

—In most cases, nomination is utterly unsystematic. There is no prescribed procedure, no recommended list of what characteristics to look for, what to weigh heavily, and what to disregard. Where standards are provided, they usually consist of vague descriptions (such as "leadership") which are subject to widely varying interpretations. The result is close to utter unpredictability; one never really knows whether different nominators are reacting to the same aspects of employee performance or even whether the same nominator uses the same standards on all occasions.

—Nomination is nearly always the view of a single individual, the employee's immediate supervisor. Although the next highest level of management is usually expected to endorse the nomination, in practice this is perfunctory. The next highest manager typically has too little experience with the nominee's abilities to make an evaluation, so he or she simply agrees with the subordinate's nomination in order to satisfy formal requirements. Consequently, nearly all nominees are viewed through one pair of eyes. However, we all tend to react primarily to certain aspects of someone else's behavior and to ignore other aspects. Therefore, limiting the base of observation to a single observer inevitably provides a narrow, not necessarily representative perspective on how the subordinate has performed.

—Managerial mythology notwithstanding, managers frequently do not know what behavioral characteristics have made for success or failure in their organization. In the absence of clear guidance on this question, they are thrown back on a combination of their own intuition and whatever mythology is generally accepted in their company. Almost inevitably, this leads to overrating certain characteristics and underrating others.

For example, personnel managers who are selected because they are likable are often criticized for reluctance to make unpopular decisions; and production managers who are selected because they get things done are likely to be criticized for harming employee morale. In both cases, the criticism is simply another aspect of the very characteristic that led to the manager being selected in the first place. The error in such cases is not one of choosing the wrong person but of having an oversimplified view of what the job really requires.

—Nomination is an unavoidably subjective process. Most organizations actually assure this subjectivity by providing little or no guidance to their nominators. The most serious disadvantages to subjectivity in nomination are that it is highly error-prone, and even more prone to accusations of bias and favoritism. Such accusations, if widely believed, can have a corrosive effect upon morale.

But even where some kind of "objective" guidance is provided, there is no feasible way to ensure that it will be used. (One large company insisted that managers substantiate their ratings by citing at least one incident in support of each rating. This was abandoned after managers claimed the system was excessively burdensome and time-consuming.) In practice, therefore, managers are free to react to whatever they like: to checklists or to intuition, to some recent example of the employee's behavior or to a stereotyped impression they may have formed of the employee months or years ago. True, some managers have excellent records of identifying promising young employees, but most do not. Indeed, in some cases, managers' nominations may tell more about their own preferences and preconceptions than about the performance of their nominees.

Despite the weaknesses, nomination is too firmly entrenched a tradition to be dispensed with; nor need it be. Methods are available which can overcome most (though not all) of its weaknesses. Specifically, it is possible to systematize the process, to use multiple rather than single evaluations, and to arm the manager with reliable knowledge of what kinds of behavior to look for. Unfortunately, we have no reliable and feasible method for ensuring that nominators are reacting to behavior rather than to stereotypes.

Systematizing the nomination process begins with the realization that for all its faults, the method "works"—at least some of the time. Organizations manage to function, grow, and prosper despite the fact that their most critical single resource—managerial talent—is selected somewhat haphazardly, especially at the lower levels, where policies are implemented. (Selection tends to be more stringent at the higher levels, where policies are made—which is perhaps the saving grace of the system.) There must, then, be insights and concepts somewhere in the organization that lead managers to valid nominations some of the time. The problem is to search out these nuggets, which tend to be scattered, and unite them in a coherent approach that can be made available to everyone.

What is needed is a means of collecting—and, in some cases, articulating—managerial insights that have proven to be valid in the past. Thus the collective wisdom of all managers in an organization can be made available to each of them. Or to put it another way, we need a way to mine and sort out what individual managers already know, so that each manager can enhance his or her own views with those of the others. A simple survey usually suffices.

The following list is a composite of several such surveys, each in a different industry. Note the behavioral, rather than descriptive, orientation. Managers are not asked to interpret or classify employees' behavior (which would thrust them into the role of psychologist, for which they are likely to be ill-prepared). Instead they are asked to function as witnesses—to state that certain actions are, or are not, characteristic of a particular employee. Note also that behavioral lists of this kind avoid a general rating. This is done to exclude, as far as possible, impressions derived from sources other than those believed to be clearly relevant. This particular list happens to be rather heavily weighted toward employees in factories, but essentially the same technique can be used for calling attention to employees with supervisory potential in any part of an organization.

A number of caveats are in order. First, this particular list is not necessarily valid in organizations other than those for which it was developed; it is included here solely as an illustration of behaviorally-based nomination aids. Second, this list specifies behavior that is deemed relevant to the question of promotion, though not necessarily to the appraisal of current performance or to such performance-related questions as salary administration. Many of the behaviors that have negative implications for a higher-level job—such as keeping to oneself or not expressing curiosity—are quite common and in no way deserving of criticism. It is possible to do one's job satisfactorily and earn every cent of one's pay without evincing any supervisory potential; indeed most employees do exactly that. But for precisely that reason (a) only certain specific aspects of everyday performance are relevant to the question of promotability, and (b) the question of promotability must be clearly distinguished from that of evaluating and rewarding current performance.

An indicated potential for effective work at a higher level should never be a criterion for evaluating the worth of one's performance at a lower level, and vice versa. While the two questions obviously overlap to some degree, they should be kept as separate as possible, not only conceptually but administratively. In this context it is helpful to remember that the great bulk of the world's work is done, and done well enough, by people who are not only not promotable but who would benefit in no way from being castigated for it. Finally, it cannot be overemphasized that the interpretations offered in the comments that follow each question are tentative and represent hypotheses for further investigation rather than reliable interpretations of any individual's behavior.

Questions to be answered by supervisors of employees
nominated for promotion

A. Does the employee usually take effective preventive or corrective action himself (herself), without having to be told?

Comment: The great majority of employees "know," in a purely intellectual sense, how to handle the various contingencies that can arise on their jobs. That is, they "know" in the sense of being able to answer a question correctly. Translating this knowledge into action is not automatic, however, simply because attention tends to wander and because actions which are easier than prescribed actions tend to become habitual. Fundamentally, the problem is not so much with employees as with work that is so organized as to make it difficult for most people to sustain their attention or to preserve correct operating habits. However, much of the world's work *is* organized this way, and for technical and financial reasons, much of it will remain so organized.

Hence it is an essential part of the supervisor's job to compensate for the effects of such jobs upon employee behavior by continually reminding employees of, and reinforcing, correct procedures. Those employees who manage to remind themselves, and who therefore need relatively little supervisory support, *are already doing part of the supervisory job*. They are remembering what is easy to forget, and they are translating that memory into action. In essence, this question selects a particular aspect of job behavior for special attention, precisely because the behavior corresponds to one of the critical requirements of effective performance in the next highest-level job.

B. Does the employee tend to seek advice or assistance to deal with problems he (she) already has enough knowledge or skill to handle?

Comment: This is normal, and even desirable, with a relatively inexperienced employee. Trainers now realize that it is not enough to tell, or even to show, the employee the correct way to handle a particular situation. Beyond merely knowing what to do (again, in the sense of being able to answer a question correctly), employees must also have confidence in their knowledge; they must be assured that their interpretation of instructions is correct, or that a particular situation is in fact an instance of the general type of problem about which instruction has been given. Thus for the inexperienced employee, some uncertainty about how classroom learning can be applied to on-the-job circumstances is quite normal. In such cases, questions to supervisors should be encouraged, since they reinforce learning and hasten the development of competence.

With experienced employees, however, continuing requests for advice or help are likely to have quite different implications. At the very least, they might suggest that an employee is slow to develop confidence in the transfer of training to experience. This in turn suggests a prolonged period of uncertainty and hesitancy to act in a higher-level job, where, by definition, one expects to encounter a greater frequency of circumstances demanding decisive action. At worst, continued seeking of guidance could be due to a reluctance to accept responsibility for one's actions. When people with this characteristic are given responsibility for decisions, they tend to become rigid, bureaucratic rule-followers. They are also likely to discover many circumstances beyond their control on which to blame any shortcomings in their department's performance, instead of seeking ways to compensate for or circumvent those circumstances.

C. Does the employee offer advice or assistance to other employees? Is such advice or help actually sought by other employees? Is the advice usually followed? Is the assistance usually accepted?

Comment: This question probes the influence the employee has on fellow employees. To the extent that the guidance is accepted— or better yet, sought and accepted—the employee is (once again) already doing part of the supervisory job. And after all, the ultimate test of leadership is whether anyone is following.

It is not uncommon for highly competent workers to keep pretty much to themselves on the job. They may be respected and even liked by their fellow employees, but if their peers do not identify them as a resource to be sought out when guidance is needed, their leadership potential must be questioned. Entirely too many unfortunate supervisory promotions have been based on job competence alone—without reference to whether peers have, in effect, "promoted" the individual already (in terms of the role they want the person to play) or whether they look elsewhere for this kind of informal leadership. Merely placing a formal mantle of authority on the shoulders of someone whom peers have not acknowledged as a leader is quite unlikely to change their reaction (or any comparable group's reaction) to that person. In such a situation we are exposed to the familiar double loss caused by unwise supervisory selections: we lose a good worker, and we get a poor supervisor.

D. Has the employee expressed interest in data or evaluations relating to his (her) own performance? Has he (she) expressed interest in the department's, division's, or plant's performance as well?

Comment: It would be sound motivational practice for supervisors to provide this kind of information routinely. (See the case of Supervisor C in Chapter 3.) Alas, it is frequently the exception rather than the rule. But in such cases, individuals who express a continuing curiosity about how well they (and their unit) are doing may be manifesting one aspect of what psychologists call the "achievement motive." Especially if the individual sets his or her own production targets and seeks the performance data chiefly to know whether they are being achieved, he or she may be predisposed to primary work satisfaction from accomplishment itself. In a supervisory role, such a person is likely to identify the department's achievements with his or her own feelings of success and failure and will therefore seek ways of helping the department to accomplish as much as it can.

On the other hand, indifference or a lack of curiosity suggests that the quality of the individual's performance may not be one of the person's prime interests. Emotional investment in the work would thus be more a matter of conforming to group patterns or following the supervisor's lead than of personal interest. Thrust into a supervisory role, such a person is likely to be more interested in following comfortable routines than in actively seeking out ways to improve the department's performance.

E. Are the employee's expressed ideas easy to understand especially to people who have different backgrounds of education or experience than he (she) has? Or are his (her) expressed ideas unclear or difficult to interpret?

Comment: This evaluation is, of course, aimed at verbal facility or "communications style." It should be based on as wide a sample of people as possible, since the fact that a supervisor understands a subordinate is no guarantee that other people do. The communication demands on supervisors are more exacting than those on subordinates, since supervisors must deal with higher levels of management and with other specialized departments in addition to their own. It is helpful, therefore, if they can make themselves understood by people who do not necessarily share a specialized vocabulary or background of experience.

As pointed out in Chapter 4, one's effectiveness as a communicator can be enhanced. But whether enhancement will succeed in any individual case is always an uncertainty. So an existing facility at making oneself understood has the merit of removing at least some of the doubt from a prediction that is already quite uncertain to begin with.

F. Does the employee work at a more or less steady rate, or are there wide variations in his (her) productivity from time to time?

Comment: Some variation in activity level is unavoidable, since the individual must respond to various outside influences, including emergencies that may demand a considerable burst of energy. There are also times when little energy is required. (A surprising amount of working time is spent waiting for work to arrive, for other people to get ready, or for a decision to be made.) But setting these aside, wide amplitude in an individual's work pace is often an expression of fluctuating moods, with the productive periods being in fact panicky efforts to catch up and the slow periods being times of distracted attention. A person whose work pace is characterized by such wide swings is likely to bring an equally inconsistent pace to a supervisory job, making the individual rather unpredictable (and also incomprehensible) to subordinates.

A steady work rate is often the result of deliberate pacing. Consciously or unconsciously, some individuals set a pace they know they can maintain, and keep to it. Such a pace almost always includes a reserve of uncommitted energy which can be used in a crisis. These people work in a steady, unfrenetic way. They are unlikely to be tired at the end of the day. Because their *average* work pace is usually greater than that of people whose pace fluctuates, they will accomplish more, and with less last-minute urgency. As supervisors, they will tend to be predictable and understandable to their subordinates, who will know what is wanted, often without having to be told.

G. Does the employee tend to revert to inefficient or incorrect procedures even after correct procedures have been pointed out to him (her)?

Comment: The two most likely explanations for such behavior are the tendency of old habits to persist and/or insufficient attention to the explanation of the correct procedure. Neither bode well for supervision, in which the individual would be expected to adapt to periodic organizational or technical changes and to discern what superiors mean with a minimum of repetition. It must also be recognized that supervisors are just as prone to falling into sloppy habits as anyone else. (See, for example, the case of Supervisor L in Chapter 3.) Therefore, the ability to extricate oneself from such habits, when they are pointed out, is a useful asset to any supervisor. On the other hand, a demonstrated tendency not to do so suggests limits on how far the individual's supervisory potential can realistically be expected to develop.

H. Does the employee rapidly adapt to unfamiliar circumstances or assimilate unfamiliar information? Does he (she) enjoy such excursions into the unfamiliar or complain about them?

Comment: This question is perhaps more pertinent to the problem of the individual's promotability beyond first-level supervision than it is for first-level supervision itself. As supervisors move into higher levels of management, they must often work with disciplines and technologies other then those in which they have been trained. However, even at the first level of supervision a major adaptation is called for; they must stop doing their old job and start supervising. Individuals who are too comfortable with the familiar to give it up and launch themselves into a learning experience—in which, by definition they will be at least temporarily inexpert—may never make this basic transition successfully. If so, they will probably be so busy stifling initiative among their subordinates that they won't have time to plan or organize their work effectively.

This question is limited, however, in that quite often employees below the supervisory level simply have no opportunity to encounter unfamiliar problems, and the question is therefore relatively useless. However, failure to provide such opportunities is itself an unwise motivational practice. Furthermore, a valuable benefit of organizing work so that a certain amount of nonroutine is encountered is that reactions to such encounters provide useful clues to supervisory potential.

I. Does the employee tend to call maintenance (or other specialists) to handle a problem that he (she) could be expected to correct without assistance?

Comment: This type of behavior is usually due to a lack of inquisitiveness about the causes of the problems encountered and/or a need for a break to relieve the monotony. Needless to say, such actions hurt productivity. Lack of curiosity is particularly damaging in supervisors, since they encounter endless problems that can be solved easily enough by a bit of clever deduction. Supervisors who automatically call for help whenever they encounter a problem are in effect functioning as little more than messengers between the department and the maintenance crew. They are also in danger of the same fate as befell the legendary boy who cried "wolf" too often; the maintenance crews resent frequent unnecessary calls and may not take them seriously when they get into real trouble.

The need for an occasional break is understandable, but using everyday contingencies as an occasion for frequent, self-determined rest periods is a habit that would ill serve a supervisor. Unlike their subordinates, supervisors are often free to go wherever they please; and during a harried day, some may seek refuge in their office or lounge while the department's operations deteriorate from trouble to chaos. One would of course prefer supervisors who can steel themselves to endure boredom or frustration until their department is back under control.

J. Does the employee keep busy during periods of smooth operation—for example, checking quality, routinely examining
potential trouble spots, assuring that adequate supplies are
available, cleaning the area, and so on?

Comment: One of the most revealing episodes in day-to-day
performance is what people do when there is "nothing to do"—
nothing that is urgent or immediately demanding. In perhaps a
majority of cases, the reaction to "nothing to do" is to do nothing.
Freed of pressing demands from their work, many people are
content to wait until the next demand arrives, knowing from
experience that it will indeed arrive. Often, however, that next
demand is something that can be anticipated or prevented if
proper vigilance is maintained. Slack periods are also ideal for
accomplishing necessary work that is too often put off to the
last minute (and therefore done badly, besides interfering with
the performance of more urgent tasks), including cleaning,
filing, record-keeping, and reading background information.

The individual who makes productive use of slack time is better
organized, and therefore less likely to lose control of the work,
than someone who uses it to rest, daydream, or gossip. By the
same token the productive individual is more likely to stay in
control of an entire department than someone who views the
job as a series of crises with welcome breathing spaces inter-
spersed between them.

Even when lists like this are used regularly, they provide no
guarantee against promotion of inadequate supervisors or
against overlooking potentially effective candidates. But the only
intelligent way to evaluate any procedure is to compare it with
its alternatives. When the alternative is the typically unstructured
system of simply asking managers to recommend candidates for
promotion, without specifying which characteristics are desirable
and without requiring any kind of substantiation of the manager's
opinion, lists of this kind cannot fail to reduce the frequency of
errors. Thus the process of nomination is rendered at least somewhat more systematic and relevant and somewhat less subjective; and for all these reasons it is more likely to search out the

best potential in an existing population and, in the process, to preserve morale.

Selection

The second way to alleviate some of the inherent weaknesses in the "promotion from within" system is by addressing the selection process itself. For a time, especially during the 1950s and 1960s, many organizations used psychological tests of various kinds for this purpose. These gradually fell out of favor due to doubts about their validity, their susceptibility to charges of discrimination, and the rise in popularity of so-called "assessment centers."

The assessment center is essentially a series of exercises which simulate various aspects of a managerial job. Candidates, usually in small groups, are asked to spontaneously play assigned roles (or, in a more interesting version, unassigned roles) in various discussions, games, and problem-solving assignments. The raw data for assessing managerial potential is their actual behavior during these exercises, as viewed simultaneously by several evaluators.

The principle underlying assessment centers is that the best predictor of behavior is behavior. Or, to put it more cumbersomely (and more accurately), the best predictor of future behavior is recent behavior in a similar setting, evaluated by the same standards that will be applied to the future job and by as many independent observers as possible. This mouthful is based on yet another principle: most people's behavior is relatively consistent in similar circumstances over reasonably long periods of time.

Granted, one may not behave in a lecture hall the way one behaves in a tavern; but over a period of months or even years a person's behavior in a lecture hall is likely to be at least roughly consistent with itself, and behavior in a tavern during the same period is likely to resemble itself most of the time. An age factor enters here. Behavior is likely to be stable over longer periods for adults in their middle or later years than for younger adults.

Therefore, assessments (or, for that matter, any form of behavior prediction) are likely to be valid over a shorter time span for younger adults than for older ones.

Perhaps the greatest difficulty in trying to forecast supervisory job performance on the basis of nonsupervisory job performance (which is essentially what nomination attempts) is that the two jobs are seldom very similar—certainly not in their more critical aspects. For this reason, by far the best method of evaluating someone's supervisory potential is to make the person an acting supervisor for an extended period, and then sit back and see what happens. Obviously, this is not a practical method in most cases. The next best approach is to screen candidates by focusing nomination on specific, relevant aspects of job performance, and then to select from among those candidates by assessment.

The assessment procedure is relatively expensive, at least in terms of time, since an entire day (preferably two) must be given up by the candidates and even more by the judges. Nevertheless, the benefits seem to be so much greater than those of alternative methods (such as tests or interviews) that the significance of the lower cost of the alternatives pales in any cost/benefit comparison. The major benefit of assessment (in addition to its apparently greater accuracy in identifying people who perform effectively in higher-level positions) is its greater acceptance by both candidates and managers. Assessment is a much closer approximation of supervisory reality than other methods, and this verisimilitude tends to reduce the objections that many people have to being evaluated or that managers have to accepting evaluations they did not make themselves. However, to balance the picture it must be noted that managers who resent having some procedure in which they do not participate as a substitute for their own personal judgments are just as miffed by the use of assessment as they are by tests or any other procedure.

Assessment seems to have four main advantages over other methods of predicting future performance.

—First, the problems which the candidates face are at least analogous to those a supervisor would face, so the observations of their behavior are relevant to the jobs for which they are being considered.

—Second, there are usually at least four simultaneous observers, so assessment benefits from the jury effect. The consensus that emerges from several viewers is usually a better prediction of other people's future evaluations of a candidate than is any one observer's prediction. (The same effect has been observed in so-called "peer evaluations." Here, the consensus of classmates' predictions of a student's future performance tends to be more accurate than predictions by the student's instructor. The jury effect of combining many views into a consensus is probably more important than the fact that the viewers are peers of the viewee.)

—Third, assessment is usually confined to prescreened candidates, so the competition is tougher. Weaknesses which might be too subtle to note when the candidate is compared with mediocre employees are likely to stand out in bold relief when he or she is compared with topflight candidates.

—Fourth, interviewees are probably more adept at "selling" themselves to interviewers than interviewers are at recognizing that they are being sold. Assessment neatly avoids this problem, since the candidates are reacting to each other rather than to the judges.

The following notes, taken from a judge's observations of candidates in one exercise at an assessment center, give some inkling as to the power of the techniques in revealing behavioral trends. The exercise in this case was a "business game" in which the candidates were asked to "operate" a fictitious company by making a series of decisions under pressure of both time and uncertainty about prices and costs. As is typical in these exercises, no one was assigned a specific role, and the group's principal problem was to organize itself, agree upon a strategy, and develop a mechanism for coping with both its own results and unexpected changes in the rules of the game.

When the game began, M spent several minutes doing some calculations on a piece of paper while everyone else was arguing heatedly about what to do. Then R asked him what he was doing, and M replied that he was figuring out the profitability of the different products they were supposed to make. R said that was a good idea and asked J and W to help M, so the calculations could be completed more quickly.

A few minutes later M was able to announce that one product had an advantage over the others with regard to rate of return. R suggested that they get to work on that product to the exclusion of others. He then asked whether anyone had a preferred role to play. No one did, so R suggested they organize themselves into an assembly line. Before they actually did so, M pointed out that it would take several precious minutes before an assembly line could reach full production, and that it might be better to organize production around two-man teams. R promptly agreed that this was a better idea. He thanked M for pointing out his error and asked if M would work with him on a production team. M agreed.

Shortly after production had begun, the "incoming mail" arrived. R was rather dismayed at how many documents had come in. M suggested that R screen the mail quickly and bring anything important to the group's attention, and that he (M) would work alone until R finished. J objected that giving the mail to one person was dangerous because he might not appreciate the importance of every document. M replied that it was more practical for one person to read the mail and that he personally had full faith in R.

R rifled quickly through the mail, noting that most of it was of little importance. He voiced a suspicion that the "mail" was merely a distraction designed to trick them into diverting manpower from production. M said that the chance of something important being included in the mail was great enough that they could not risk ignoring it. Then R discovered a letter from a "customer," objecting to the fact that the very product they were making was priced too high and "threatening" to seek another supplier if a substantial discount were not granted. R immediately realized that either the discount or the loss of the customer's business would drastically alter the profitability of the product. He suggested that production work be suspended while the group considered the problem.

J again objected, saying that they were only just beginning to get into a good working pace. Just then the bell rang, signaling the end of a "month," and the judges immediately posted price changes for both products and parts. J accused R of having led the group down a blind alley by concentrating on a single, vulnerable product. R was clearly under attack. J was trying to remove him from leadership. W tended to support his teammate J. M busied himself studying the new figures, while the two other candidates, S and T, pleaded for calm and restraint.

R then pointed out that changes like these were likely to continue throughout the game, and that rather than locking themselves into any one strategy, as they had initially done, they needed a mechanism for evaluating changes so they could react in a quick, orderly way whenever it was necessary. He proposed that one of them be detached from productive work to analyze price and profit trends and to scan the mail. He said that so far M had clearly shown himself to be the best analyst in the group, so he nominated him for this role. He also recommended that the two other production teams continue to operate, and that he (R) serve as a messenger, rushing completed "products" to the "bank," purchasing "parts" with the proceeds, and rushing these back to the production teams where they were needed.

J now made his most serious challenge, saying that R was trying to appoint himself leader of the group and that he hadn't heard anyone else agree to that. R replied that he was perfectly willing to change roles with J, to work on a production team with W while J served as the messenger. The important thing, he stressed, was not who did what but whether the group was organized so as to be able to cope with more unexpected changes of the kind that had already caused them so much trouble. W then acknowledged that R's ideas made sense and asked J to remain on the production team with him, since they had already proven that they could work well together. J, recognizing that he had not gained support for his attack on R and that R's views were accepted by the others, quietly agreed.

From that point forward the teams worked smoothly. M became adroit at figuring out how to take advantage of price and cost changes, and R served as a communications link and an effective source of help. The group's final "profit" figure ranked in the top 30 percent of similar groups playing this game.

Exercises of this kind last about two hours, and there are three or four of them per day in a typical assessment center. Behavior in any one exercise is not necessarily typical of the individual, but when someone tends to play essentially the same role in one unstructured session after another, it is reasonable to assume that a persistent aspect of personality is being tapped. Further, this aspect is likely to characterize behavior in similar situations, at least in the near future. This is the logic on which performance predictions from assessment center behavior are based.

In the above case, R's contribution was not so much recognizing what needed to be done as recognizing M's superiority at making analyses. He suggested a division of labor, which until that time had occurred to no one; and he successfully defended his ideas against J's charge that he was trying to usurp power for himself. On the other hand, his initial enthusiasm for narrowly-based strategy very nearly led the group into serious trouble, although he was strong enough to admit it and quickly recognized how to avoid that trap thereafter.

M was perhaps the wisest of the candidates, but he did not communicate his ideas well and needed the intercession of R to have an impact on the group. Events usually proved M's views to have been correct, but it was unlikely that he would have persuaded the others of this before the proof came in, or for that matter that he would even have tried to persuade them. He and R made an excellent combination, each buttressing the other's weakness; but it took R to recognize this.

J was perhaps the most socially sensitive of the candidates. He saw that R had seized de facto leadership, and he recognized when R was vulnerable to attack. But he had no real alternative program to offer, and his attempt to capitalize on the group's initial bewilderment when R admitted his error did little but temporarily divide the group—and offer R his chance to demonstrate that he could put the group's interests above his own.

W, S, and T, the other candidates, were more active than these excerpted notes would make it appear. However, in terms of influencing the productivity of others—which, after all, is the essence of the supervisory job for which all six candidates were being assessed—R and M were more effective than the others.

Some Inescapable Problems

Attempts to make promotion less haphazard have their costs, some of which are both inescapable and uncomfortable. Here we will consider three such problems: (1) whether these systems "homogenize" supervision to the detriment of the organizations that use them, (2) whether they tend to produce "heirs apparent" to the detriment of other aspirants to promotion, and (3) whether the effects of such systems on those who are not promoted are excessively harmful.

One of the stickiest questions about systematizing the promotion process is whether it locks the organization into a particular leadership style. In other words, will any "system" necessarily narrow the range of leadership styles? And will that narrowing be to the organization's benefit—especially in the long run?

Any systematic approach to personnel selection tends to narrow the range of behavior predispositions in the selected group, as compared to the larger population from which it was chosen. That is precisely what a selection system is designed to do. In practice, the narrowing is achieved not so much by selecting those who fit a stereotype as by reducing the number who are unlikely to reach a certain standard.

For example, in the assessment center case cited above, if we could assume that performance in this particular exercise was characteristic of all of the candidates (which we *cannot* ever assume of any one exercise), the effect of selection would probably be to exclude W, S, and T from the ranks of supervisors. This would be done because they had a minimal influence on the behavior of others in the group. They were good team workers and collaborated well with the other candidates, but they exerted little or no steering or decision influence on the others. They were thus displaying characteristics which are highly desirable in workers and which may, in fact, have impressed their superiors favorably enough to recommend that they be considered for assessment. But they were giving no evidence of the *sine qua non* of supervision, which is influence upon other people's behavior. By excluding these individuals from supervision, the selection system would narrow the range of supervisory style by winnowing out some styles deemed ineffective.

So the answer to the first sticky question—does systematizing the promotion process narrow the range of leadership styles?—

is yes. But the narrowing does not *necessarily* result in a homogenized leadership style for all supervisors. If that happens at all, it is much more likely to result from informal "training" by older supervisors and the inculcation of certain preferred approaches by higher management, over a period of years.

The second question is even stickier: Is *any* narrowing of supervisory styles desirable in the long run? The answer depends in part on what is meant by the *long run.* Certainly in the foreseeable future (the limited range of years that will be heavily influenced by events that have already occurred and that is therefore at least somewhat predictable) we will still need supervisors whose primary function is to influence the way in which subordinates do their work. Beyond that brief range the future is dim; but precisely because we cannot anticipate it, there is little sense in basing plans on assumptions about it.

A more practical (hence more difficult) question is: Do we know enough about the relationship of supervisory styles to organizational requirements to be able to determine which styles will be more effective than others, even in the foreseeable future? After all, there are many ways of influencing behavior: fear, example, persuasion, appeals to pride, loyalty, avarice, and so on. Surely the mere fact that someone can get others to act more or less as he wishes is not, in itself, an indication of *effective* supervision—if effectiveness means that the long-range beneficial effects outweigh the long-range detrimental effects.

The evidence seems to favor three generalizations about supervisory style, all of which can be built in as criteria for a systematic approach to supervisory selection:

—Supervisory styles that tend to demean the dignity or self-esteem of subordinates, such as threats of firing or severe castigation, tend to reduce productivity and in some cases to foment rebellion (strikes, sabotage). The only "advantage" of these styles is that they usually get a quick response.

—Styles that support or enhance subordinates' self-respect, such as increasing their authority in accordance with their knowledge, and using mistakes as teaching opportunities rather than as exercises for berating, tend to raise both productivity and employee responsiveness to urgent needs or sudden pressures.

—Styles that are flexible and respond appropriately to employee behavior—praising that which is praiseworthy, criticizing that which is wrong, giving help or advice where it is needed and abstaining where it is not—are likely to be more effective in the long run than styles which follow a rigid pattern (always praising or always criticizing) regardless of circumstances.

(Note that there is no conflict between supportive and flexible styles. To praise or quietly tolerate a consistent abuser of privileges or a consistent nonperformer is not supportive but coddling. There is, alas, a persistent canard, perpetuated by management writers who should know better, that supportive supervision means not only letting subordinates get away with murder but congratulating them for it. This is, of course, absurd; the supportive supervisor supports the egos of employees who respond maturely to such support and does not indulge those few who abuse it.)

In the foreseeable future, organizations will be better off if they narrow supervisory styles along these lines. As for the unforeseeable future, some other author, perhaps unborn, will have to write about that when it begins to make itself apparent.

The problem of "heirs apparent" (individuals who are singled out for seemingly inevitable advancement to higher positions) is not peculiar to systematic promotion schemes. Long before there were standardized nominations or assessment centers, there were bosses' sons and bosses' favorites. Further, the tendency for persons of outstanding ability and motivation to distinguish themselves early, through exceptional performance, is probably as old as organizations themselves.

In brief, the problem of heirs apparent has been around for a long time. Some of its reasons for existence are regarded today as reprehensible (favoritism), some as laudible (achievement). Much of the regard is in the eye of the beholder; the disappointed office-seeker sees things differently than the successful one. Whether the systematic selection procedures aggravate, or simply inherit, the age-old problem of heirs apparent depends on whether the system is perceived as equitable and on whether it seems susceptible to manipulation.

Promotion systems (even those that aren't "systems" at all but merely habits) do not affect everyone's ego. A surprising number of nonmanagers have no interest in ever becoming managers. But those egos that are affected by promotion systems tend to be the biggest, tenderest, most easily wounded egos in the organization. To minimize the wounds, organizations have to support, explain, and sometimes defend their promotion systems. Few do. Hence the problem of heirs apparent being bitterly resented by unsuccessful rivals is more ubiquitous than it need be.

No great "selling" skill is needed to support a promotion system. What is needed, however, is a system that is as fair as humanly possible and that is administered as scrupulously as the organization can manage. With this kind of basis, efforts to explain and support the system have a good chance of mollifying all but the most recalcitrant objectors.

Even where no one quarrels with the choices that are made, disappointment is inevitable, and sometimes excruciating, for unsuccessful candidates who know they were being considered. This is one of the costs of assessment, since the fact of candidacy can hardly be concealed from assessees. However, the less obvious forms of selection, in which only the successful candidates have unequivocal evidence of consideration, merely postpone the problem. It must eventually dawn on people who begin to see less experienced employees promoted above them that they have been bypassed, and that the only future they have to look forward to is an indefinite repetition of the present. The pill is no less bitter if it melts slowly in the mouth than if it is swallowed whole.

Disappointments with regard to promotion are inevitable in any hierarchy. In pyramidal organization, the mathematical chances of further promotion decrease every time one is promoted. We must therefore ask whether the problem of disappointment is frequent enough, and severe enough, to curtail the use of procedures, such as assessment, that make candidacy obvious.

Frequent—perhaps. Severe—no. Most adults are tough enough to withstand worse blows than disappointment without lasting damage. This is not to suggest that the experience isn't painful but only that most people can go right on functioning despite the pain. Most egos—even the big, tender ones—are resilient and mature enough to take this kind of disappointment with a few grumbles and let it go at that. The fact that some people will inevitably dislike the effects that open candidacy for promotion has upon them is not reason enough to curtail the practice. The benefits outweigh the costs.

Chapter 6
Development

For many years, adult learning capacity was regarded as more or less fixed. A person was only so smart and would never be smarter; and barring senility or some other neurological damage, that person would never be dumber either. Today we are no longer as sure of the immutability of adult intelligence as we once were.

Recent experimental work with children indicates that quite remarkable changes in the level of apparent intelligence, or adaptive responses to the environment, are possible. For evidently ill-adapted children who do not suffer from damaged nervous systems, a behavior pattern of apathy and unresponsiveness may be a normal, and reversible, reaction to an uninteresting, unrewarding environment. If such a child can be removed quickly enough from an environment that lacks interesting things and placed in an environment that offers opportunities for some kind of personal success, there is a chance that the passive, "unintelligent" behavior will be replaced by an adaptive, coping, "intelligent" pattern of behavior.

Whether there is an analogy in adult learning has not been fully established. We do know that normal and even above-normal adults, after years of immersion in stultifying organizational environments where the learning potential is quickly mined out, may give strong superficial indications of no longer being able to learn. Sometimes, but not always, this apparent arrest of learning can be reversed by changing the environment. In any case, it is much easier to prevent the arrest of adult learning than to try to resuscitate it.

We will use the term *development* to refer to learning that takes place independently of instruction—what one learns from doing, from observing, and from thinking about one's experiences. Development accounts for the lion's share of adult learning, because adults have fewer classroom opportunities and more developmental opportunities than children. At least, the more fortunate do.

The practical importance of development can scarcely be overstated. Yet it has received far less attention from educators and policy makers than the more familiar (and less critical) classroom type of education. It is development that determines whether individuals will ever have more competence than can be given by a teacher or a textbook—whether they can ever rise above the limits of what was known when they were students, of what their teachers were able to teach, and of what they were motivated to learn during their most immature and unsophisticated years. It is development that determines whether raw potential and the ability to verbalize concepts are ever transformed into functional, sophisticated competence.

In organizational terms, it is development, not formal training, that determines whether an organization will be able to staff itself with managers, specialists, and technicians. These are the people whose efforts are critical in keeping the organization technically capable and economically competitive. Most large organizations invest heavily (and, let it be clearly noted, necessarily) in formal training programs for employees in these jobs. The pity of it is that much less time and effort is expended on development—the effort to ensure that training neither withers away nor becomes the limiting factor on what the individual can actually do.

Classrooms are efficient devices for teaching vocabularies, nomenclatures, and the processing and communicating of information. They lend themselves to teaching concepts and verbal responses to verbally-presented problems. They can be used for teaching manual and instrumental skills, although under conditions which by definition are at best approximations of those existing on the job.

However, classrooms cannot teach wisdom, subtle cues to look for, and "tricks of the trade." They cannot teach what theorists have not yet theorized or what researchers have not yet discovered. Above all, they cannot teach confidence—a reasonable degree of certainty that a specific contingency is in fact an example of a general one discussed in the classroom, or that the remedy the neophyte thinks should be applied is in fact the correct one under the circumstances. All these things are learned, if they are learned at all, in development.

In any individual case, development is a function of the capacity for learning and the kinds of experience to which a person is exposed. When development has been inadequate to meet an organization's needs, the most common explanation given by the organization is that the capacity is lacking. In other words, the individual was originally recruited to fill a position whose requirements were so much lower than those of more advanced positions that the individual's learning ability was simply unable to close the gap. Another common explanation is that the individual represents a selection error, that the person's ability to develop was overrated at the time of hiring. Either explanation could be correct, but both are given far too glibly and frequently to fit the facts.

More often than we care to admit, employees of long standing who are considered unlikely to learn to cope effectively with any higher-level job (who are too "undeveloped") do not suffer from inadequate talent but from ruined talent. Management has (no doubt inadvertently) exploited the employees' initial level of development for too long, without providing further developmental opportunities. Individuals who have learned, then relearned, and finally overlearned their job, to the exclusion of having to face new challenges, are in acute danger of working without thinking, without curiosity or alertness, without interest in experimentation or variation. Their development is unlikely to have proceeded very far beyond whatever high-water mark it had reached when they were first introduced to their present job. Superficially, they will give the appearance of having absorbed all the learning they can. In companies with benevolent managements, they are prime targets for bypassing. In companies that are not so benevolent, they are exposed to demotion, involuntary early retirement, or permanent layoff.

Partly to prevent such tragedies, and partly to make more effective use of the human resources in which they necessarily invest so heavily (wages, salaries, and benefits may account for very high percentages of total operating costs), sophisticated managements have increasingly attempted to foster the developmental process. These attempts have been aimed primarily at the development of managers, since this is the group in which the most acute shortages are felt. However, essentially the same principles govern the development of technicians and professional workers. Therefore, while the discussion that follows dwells particularly on management development, it should be borne in mind that with very few exceptions the title of most other key jobs could be substituted for *management* with little, if any, loss of validity.

Management Development

Management is essentially a set of skills involving the application of certain principles. The principles can be taught to or inferred by the individual, but their application can only be learned. I can teach you the principles of swimming, but you will not learn to swim until you get into the water and find your own way of using those principles. Similarly, management principles can be taught, but the only way of learning to use them is by trying to manage.

Large organizations have obvious advantages over smaller ones with respect to formal "management development" programs. They have larger training budgets, can more easily spare managerial time for course attendance, and are usually more sophisticated in selecting potential managers and course materials. However, smaller organizations have no disadvantage with regard to structuring themselves so that development is likely to occur. Thus, even if a company cannot afford large-scale investments to *train* its managers, it need not despair of *developing* them.

The conditions under which development is likely to occur in any organization are known, and it is largely futile to expect much development to occur in the absence of those conditions. Basically, managers must be assigned work that is instructive in itself, and their superiors must be charged with exploiting the instructional potential occurring in the normal course of that work. In other words, the supervisors of a developing manager must be prepared to act as coaches, not offering advice unless it is asked for but ready to discuss the pros and cons of alternative methods after the results of the manager's actions have become clear. The function of the coach is to broaden the experience of the manager by introducing aspects the person might not yet have noticed. In this way, the manager (provided, of course, he or she is wise enough to listen) can generalize from personal experience more broadly and more quickly than would otherwise be possible.

Of course, instruction, whether of the coaching or classroom variety, is unlikely to be converted to useful learning unless there is a prompt opportunity to practice what has been taught. For work to be instructive, therefore, it must contain components which occur fairly frequently and which the individual has not yet mastered. A job can teach to the extent that the jobholder has not yet run into his or her own limits of learning or the job's limits of teaching. In brief, jobs teach only by confronting individuals with what they do not know and have not mastered. Therefore, "experts" are by definition in danger of developing no further than they already have.

Our attention is naturally drawn to our own attempts to cope with a problem, and the lessons in those attempts impress themselves naturally upon our memories. In the absence of problems demanding solution our attention ordinarily wanders, and the results of those wanderings seldom add much to our store of knowledge. As a rule, we learn only when we have to, when a satisfactory response to the situation in which we find ourselves is not already within our repertoire.

This principle has two important implications.

—Very little development can be expected on the basis of a simple desire to develop. Therefore, attempts to develop managers through selection of people with a strong personal drive to expand their managerial skills, or by encouraging such a desire with inspirational messages, are likely to have limited success at best.

—Very little development can be expected to occur on a convenient schedule. Most promotions are timed to meet the organization's needs rather than the individual's growth rate. As a result, they often occur after an individual has passed the peak of readiness. Similarly, the principles taught in training courses are most likely to be applied if opportunities to do so occur shortly after they are taught. But the courses are usually scheduled at the convenience of the training department, and managers are released for training at the convenience of their superiors. Thus the relationship between the timing of training and the opportunity to practice it is usually random; for precisely this reason, much training is wasted.

Development is a manageable process in the sense that, to a reasonable degree, we can plan, organize, and control most of the variables that affect it. That is, we can identify the elements that need to be monitored (principally the length of time the individual has been in an essentially unchanged job and the degree of proficiency the person has attained); we can deploy the necessary resources for dealing with them (such as temporary assignments in unfamiliar areas, service on a task force with specialists from other areas, changes in responsibilities, and even formal training courses—if their contents can be applied relatively soon); and we can intervene in a timely way to ensure that the process is not blocked. In practice, these interventions are the most difficult part of managing development, since they tend to be opposed by managers who are not prepared to jeopardize the short-term goals by which they are measured for the sake of enhancing the long-term growth of their subordinates.

It is easy to overstate the manageability of development, which is far from a predictable process. Many of the variables involved are difficult to define, much less control (for example, the relationship between the individual and his or her boss, peers, and subordinates). For this reason, attempts to reduce the developmental process to a bureaucratic routine of filling out forms are never realistic. A certain humility is called for—a recognition that while we can increase the chances that development will occur, there is no guarantee that it actually will, at least in the way that we have planned. We can draw an apt analogy between manufacturing and farming.

In manufacturing we assume that most of the variables affecting the result we wish to achieve are, or can be put, under our control. In agriculture we assume that few of these variables are, or can be, under our control. In manufacturing our strategy is to design a system with all the appropriate controls we need. In agriculture we try to influence as much as possible those few variables we can control, in the hope that nature will be reasonably cooperative with all the other variables. Thus the plant manager can, for example, control temperature and humidity if needed, but the farmer can only pray for the right amount of rain.

The organization that wants to develop its managerial talent is in fact much closer to the farming situation and is better served by the farmer's strategies. Its objectives, therefore, are simply to create conditions in which good men and women are likely to grow naturally, and then hope that they will. This is a disappointing formula for those who perpetually hope to get results by "doing something"; but surely there is a lesson for us in the fact that so many of the "somethings" we have done to develop managers have turned out to be fads.

What follows is a description of an essentially "agricultural" approach: creating conditions in which learning from experience is likely to occur. Whether it succeeds in assuring its supply of competent managers depends far more on how it runs its business—on whether it becomes, in addition to its other missions, a talent farm—than on the use of formal training programs. Four particular aspects of how an organization runs its business are relevant to whether it also succeeds in becoming a talent farm: organization structure, job design, career planning, and control systems.

Organization Structure

The number and content of jobs, the number of levels of decision-making authority, and the division of projects into assigned responsibilities—organization structure—are inevitably an expression of management's assumptions about how the talent avail able to it is best utilized. Once embedded in that structure, the assumptions tend to become self-fulfilling prophecies. Both job performance and personal development are limited to the confines of the experiences provided within the structure, and this evidence is taken as confirmation of the wisdom inherent in its design. Changes are therefore hard to induce, because organization structures generate their own (sometimes spurious) appearance of inevitability.

An organization can be confining or liberating with respect to development. The confining effect is usually unintentional and unrecognized, because a structure is seldom designed with developmental consequences in mind. A confining organization recruits employees who have abilities that rapidly reach the levels demanded by their jobs and who then are left with no way to grow. In such organizations, movement into more demanding jobs, or simply different jobs, takes place only through attrition. As a result, there is always more talent looking for expression than there are vehicles available for that expression.

While a few fortunate individuals manage to burst the bonds imposed by a confining organization structure, most do not. They eventually adapt themselves to the lack of learning opportunities by ceasing to learn; and if they are subsequently considered for promotion, they are likely to be dismissed as unequal to it. Tragically, many of them may have been out of the learning mode for so long that they are unlikely to reenter it successfully. Thus a confining organization structure curtails or prevents the development of the people who staff it for the sake of maximizing its own convenience and minimizing its disruption.

By contrast, a liberating organization structure endures the inconvenience of frequent changes for the sake of building a surplus of highly developed people. It does not regard jobs as ends in themselves but as multipurpose structures, charged not only with getting the assigned work done well but also with developing their incumbents. A liberating organization does not function smoothly. It demands a great deal of flexibility from those who manage. Working in a liberating organization can be quite upsetting for people who need sameness and predictability to feel comfortable. On the other hand, liberating organizations can accomplish more (albeit in fits and starts) than comparable confining organizations. More importantly, they produce an invaluable by-product: people whose abilities are substantially greater than those they were hired with or given through training.

The ideal structure for developmental purposes is a small, self-contained unit which requires little or no external support and which has an undivided responsibility for the attainment of some major organizational purpose. The more the unit conforms to this task force form, the more likely are the employees to encounter experiences from which they can learn. Unfortunately, the obverse is not only true but more common. Centralizing work of given types in specialized departments regardless of which major project that work applies to (functional organization) may have certain advantages, but development is not one of them.

The task force is in effect a miniature version of the larger organization of which it is a part. But its internal communication lines are much shorter, permitting faster response and easier checking to be sure that messages are understood. The small task force develops managerial generalists because it cannot afford specialists. Lacking depth in any given function, these generalists more than compensate by showing through direct, everyday experience how actions taken in one part of the organization enhance or inhibit actions taken in other parts. The parochial regard of each function for its own work, to the comparative disregard of the organization's larger purposes—so common and so damaging in large, functionally specialized organizations—hardly has a chance to develop in a task force situation.

Service in a task force provides managers with an opportunity to learn the most essential leadership skill: the fine art of making other people effective. By contrast, their colleagues in a larger unit are more likely to encounter the wall of misunderstanding and sheer ignorance that functional organization builds between its components. Task force managers are also far less likely to develop the view that other components are unwise or unnecessary or both—a view that would not serve them well should they ever be elevated to top management levels.

Another advantage of the smaller unit is that everyone is near the top, which virtually eliminates the problem of unrecognized talent. The two major obstacles to talent recognition in a large organization—visibility and sponsorship—are obviated. The ability of the organization to identify its more promising managers early in their careers is maximized.

The principal limit on the feasibility of task force organization is management's readiness to depart from tradition. By breaking the large pyramidal organization into what is in effect a loosely linked network of small pyramids, even organizations of substantial size can become hothouses of managerial development at little or no sacrifice of operating efficiency. But the power of tradition to dampen managerial enthusiasm for otherwise attractive innovations should not be minimized. As any consultant knows, the most likely question to be asked when a client is seriously interested in an unorthodox proposal is: "Which other companies are already doing that?" The reason for this timidity can be found in the following anecdote.

A manufacturer of machine tools decided to enter a market that had been dominated for quite some time by a much larger company. The smaller company felt that their product could hold its own with that of the larger competitor and that they should be able to carve out a profitable share of the market for themselves. Sales were disappointing, however. When management investigated, the salesmen told them of their frustration in trying to combat what they called the "customer anxiety syndrome."

Purchasing agents often preferred the smaller company's products; however, they continued to order the competitor's product largely to protect themselves. Their reasoning went like this: "If we order the smaller company's machine, and it fails to meet expectations, we'll be accused of ordering an unknown machine when a well-known, reliable one is available. If we order the larger company's machine, and it fails in some way, we'll be safe from criticism. After all, we will have ordered the best-known machine with the best reputation in the market."

The greatest barrier to the adoption of conceptually attractive innovations is not fear that they are likely to fail; instead it is fear of having no adequate defense against criticism in the event (however unlikely) that they ever do fail. This is an organizational fact of life which explains the similarity of many employee-related policies to each other; it also explains the relative handful of companies in which innovations are common. Ironically, the reason innovations are easy in those few fortunate companies is that innovating, in their liberating internal environments, is the conformist thing to do.

Job Design

We ordinarily think that the purpose of a particular job is to get the work that is assigned to it done, and we therefore design jobs with strictly operational objectives in mind. But jobs have another purpose—the development of their incumbents. The proportion of managerial jobs whose primary function is development should increase at every level of authority and should reach 100 percent no lower than the level immediately below the chief executive.

A job stimulates development when some of its responsibilities have *not* been mastered. This is why the "more seasoning in the present position" prescription of many executives for the development of their subordinates can easily be a fallacy. It is also why investigative, troubleshooting, consulting, or teaching assignments can be among the most significant developmental experiences in a person's career.

Jobs contribute to the development of their incumbents under certain conditions, and it is to the advantage of the organization to create such conditions.

—First, the individual has not yet mastered the job—and knows it.

—Second, mastery of the job is within the person's capabilities, and he or she has enough optimism to at least hope that this is true.

—Third, achieving that mastery is more likely to lead to new learning opportunities than to long spells of practicing what has long since been mastered, and the individual knows it.

This reasoning runs contrary to conventional wisdom in two respects. One is the problem of what to do about managerial *mistakes,* and the other concerns the desirability of developing *experts.*

One of the tacit principles underlying the design of most jobs is the avoidance of errors. This is done (1) by excluding responsibilities that even approach the limits of the incumbent's abilities and (2) by a system of checks through which superiors review—and presumably detect any errors in—a subordinate's work. Obviously, to design jobs so they are not mastered is to court errors.

In practice, however, errors may go undetected for months or even forever, simply because thorough checks of a manager's work are seldom feasible. Also, the evaluation of many managerial decisions (especially when their consequences may take months or years to unfold) is necessarily subjective. In other words, whether it is an error or a farsighted coup may depend on who does the evaluating and on when it is done. In sum, errors are not necessarily easy or even desirable to avoid.

A case can even be made in favor of errors. Nothing is quite so instructive, chastening, or memorable as the error from which one is encouraged to learn rather than to hide. The consequences of most errors are less than catastrophic—unless they are made dangerous to careers, in which case the errors are likely to be hidden and to accumulate insidiously.

What happens to executive control when jobs are designed to be at least partially unmastered, and errors are the basis for instruction rather than punishment? Obviously, it changes, but it certainly isn't dismantled. The fine line between putting the organization in jeopardy and precluding the development of the manager is approached less timidly than it usually is. The risk of error is knowingly increased (a fine example of the "calculated risk") as the price of accelerating development.

Many of the so-called "glamour companies" that grew very rapidly during the 1960s benefited, albeit unwittingly, from this principle. The main limiting factor on growth was the availability of qualified managers. All the other elements—the markets, the demand, the manufacturing capacity, even the money—were there. Timidly at first, these companies began to advance relatively inexperienced men to middle-level positions, if for no other reason than that the only alternative to taking a chance on these untried young men was not to grow at all. (Industry-wide talent shortages precluded the large-scale use of outside recruiting.) When they performed well, bolder promotions were made, even including some senior management promotions for men who were still in their thirties.

Presently, management came to realize that the success of their younger managers was not just a piece of extraordinary good luck. Instead, they had stumbled onto a vitally important discovery: that senior levels of responsibility do not necessarily require much seniority. Further, the process of assigning capable young people to significant levels of responsibility quite early in their careers actually accelerates their development still further. Willy-nilly, the growth companies became talent farms. Far from restricting their growth, the availability of managerial talent became one of the principle forces that pushed their growth.

As the growth of these companies leveled off in the 1970s (which is mathematically inevitable with *any* exponential growth) some of them found themselves with an embarrassment of riches. They had a surplus of highly developed (and, by the same token, still developing) managerial talent. The result was more or less inevitable: departure in sizable numbers by managers too impatient to wait their turn in a period of necessarily slower growth.

Many of them were snapped up eagerly by companies which had not succeeded in generating an adequate supply of executive talent from internal sources. Others tended to move to smaller companies, where the route to the top was shorter and therefore faster. In effect, the growth companies had been talent farms not only for themselves but for the rest of industry as well.

However, most observers agree that the gain has been well worth the price. Developing people are highly motivated and more than pay their own way while they are members of an organization—provided that they stay for at least a few years, which the great majority of them do. And, of course, the company that enjoys large numbers of developing employees is in the best possible position to identify those whom it is especially anxious to keep, and, as a rule, to keep as many as it needs. Thus the losses, while painful, are seldom damaging.

Returning to the calculated risk with regard to possible errors by developing employees, the main practical problem for the manager is exactly where to draw the line. At what point is the potential error too great to be risked? When does the risk of organizational loss outweigh the desirability of helping an employee develop? This is inherently a subjective decision, and too often it is made under the worst possible conditions—quickly, under pressure, and with only fragmentary information. Under these circumstances, it is easy to compromise the policy of encouraging development for the sake of allegedly "practical" considerations that are seldom subject to adequate review.

Like any decision on supervisory intervention, this one is best made in advance. The various conditions that are likely to be encountered can be weighed and analyzed, and the conditions for intervention can be specified. Ideally, these should be disclosed to the developing subordinates, so they can know when to expect (or call for) help and when they are on their own. In any case, when common contingencies arise, supervisors who have thought through the question of the intervention point in advance have a much easier task than those who prefer to deal intuitively with every crisis that comes along. All they have to do is establish whether the existing conditions fit the criteria for intervention. If the criteria fit, they intervene. If the criteria do not fit, then despite the heat of the moment and the urgent pressures that may arise, they let the subordinate handle the situation—keeping a close eye on it but remaining quite clearly on the sidelines.

Thinking contingencies through in advance and abiding by one's decisions about when not to intervene are both very demanding tasks. That is part of the explanation for the difficulty many organizations have in trying to operate as talent farms. No matter how carefully one may assess a crisis when it is only potential or abstract, a real one can arouse panic and cause all the carefully-reasoned criteria for intervention to be thrown to the winds. Some managers have found it useful to draw an analogy between the question of when to intervene and the concept of "control" in skiing. To ski in control means to be able to stop if necessary. To manage in "enough" control means to know enough of what a subordinate is doing to be able to prevent truly catastrophic errors. The rest are the subordinate's problem— and opportunity to learn. In evaluating the subordinate's performance, the superior is more concerned by any recurrent errors than with the number that occur once. Indeed, an absence of errors in an unmastered job is cause for alarm; the subordinate may be sticking too timidly to the rulebook to learn anything but the rules.

The desirability of experts is a hardy old fallacy that is likely to linger on more because it satisfies emotional needs than because of major benefits to the organization. An "expert," if there is such a thing, is someone who knows a job too well to make an error and who presumably acquires the expertise through long service in the same job. In other words, experts first master their job and then overlearn it, *ad infinitum*, until they can do the work flawlessly without even thinking about it.

That, of course, is the fallacy. Long service in an essentially unchanged job is likely to lead to thoughtlessness, blindness to new developments, and resistance to change. In the absence of the necessity to learn, most people just stop learning. This doesn't mean that we must rush someone off to a new job the moment the old one is mastered (even if that is feasible). We can safely reap the rewards of our development and training investments for a while—but not indefinitely.

The emotional needs that experts satisfy are those of the executives whose policies create them: first, a bogus sense of security, as if one were really surrounded by infallible lieutenants; second, an easy rationalization for keeping people where they are when it is inconvenient or risky to move them.

Career Planning

While it is obviously fatuous to attempt to plan anyone's career very far into the future, it is equally fatuous not to do so for the foreseeable future. In the case of managers, this usually extends into the three-to-five year range. Within that period it will probably be desirable to introduce some major modification into the manager's job, because within that period the person will probably master the present job and return an ample dividend on the organization's training investment.

It is also obvious that most of those modifications cannot be promotion, in the sense of giving the manager authority over more assets and/or people than he or she previously had. Fortunately, development can proceed without promotion (although not without reward; pay and status indicators should signal the successful closing of a career phase and entry into a new one). The modification can be the addition of a new responsibility, the replacement of old responsibilities, or even a complete change of responsibilities.

The aim is always to confront the manager with a new learning opportunity. In a larger sense the aim is to convert the management team to a learning group and to convert the managerial career into a license or mandate to learn. Responsibilities are deliberately shifted among jobs or sought in hitherto untried activities.

Sometimes the main reason for denying a developmental opportunity to a promising manager is that it is already "taken" by someone else who is performing adequately and has no immediate prospects of promotion. This raises the delicate, and therefore seldom-faced, question of whether the organization "owes" a managerial job to anyone, and if so whether first-come-first-served is the most appropriate principle to apply. The problem is especially acute in closely held or family-owned companies, in which the roles of ownership and management are often commingled.

If the organization is committed to ensuring its supply of managers by developing them internally, it must regard managerial jobs as learning opportunities; and in that sense it cannot "owe" them to anyone. No cut-and-dried formulas are possible here, but there clearly will be occasions when a manager whose performance has been perfectly adequate will be asked to relinquish responsibilities to someone who can benefit from the learning opportunity inherent in that job. Such changes are made immeasurably easier if the organization has established (or, if necessary, decreed) a policy of "tours of duty" for middle and top level jobs.

This concept is already well-established for overseas management assignees and for military officers. Relief from the assignment marks the end of the incumbent's expected contribution to it and the completion of what that person undertook to do; there are no implications of failure. The concept has much to recommend it, but its implications for top management must be faced squarely. A tour of duty system is viable only in a reasonably fluid organization, where managers relieved from one job are accommodated in vacancies created by relieving still other managers. Insistence by top executives on retaining their own assignments indefinitely retards the flow of reassigned managers below them and can even render the entire system ineffective. In other words, the tour of duty concept may make inevitable the confrontation between the long-range interests of the organization as a whole and the individual interests of some of its leaders. It must be conceded that large organizations, because they have so many possible assignments among which to shunt their managers, have a distinct advantage over small companies in the application of the tour of duty principle.

Control Systems

In a traditional organization the control function of a superior is to make sure that subordinates are doing their jobs as it was planned that they should be done. This responsibility is not abandoned when the organization accepts the responsibility for enhancing the development of its managers, but the emphasis upon it is brought into balance with an emphasis on seeing to it that subordinates are learning from their jobs.

In practice this means that the subordinate's decisions are discussed, rather than prescribed or proscribed, and that while the superior will offer advice upon request, he or she is more likely to be alarmed than flattered by an excess of requests. Both the superior manager and the subordinate manager have new roles to learn if the latter is to grow into something more than a carbon copy of the former.

Learning new roles is never easy, but it is easi*er* when individuals see more clear-cut advantages for themselves if they do learn them. For this reason it must be noted that superiors are not only more likely to find their new roles more difficult to learn (because there is less personal advantage in it for them than there is for their subordinates) but their reluctance to adapt themselves to a coaching/controlling role will inevitably inhibit the development of many subordinates.

The process of conversion from controlling roles to coaching/controlling roles is subtle, delicate, and too easily frustrated by undersupport. With rare exceptions, undersupport of development programs is not the result of a deliberate desire to wreck them but is incidental to some other managerial purpose, such as meeting this year's production quotas or completing some ongoing project. The most common cause of undersupport is the problem of priorities.

Managers are commonly asked to support many long-range projects (of which the development of their subordinates is probably only one) while simultaneously achieving many short-term results as well. In most cases the executives who assign both sets of goals consider them not only attainable but compatible; that is, the achievement of one should not interfere with the achievement of the other. Understandably, however, the managers charged with accomplishing all of these goals do not necessarily agree. Hence they tend to give priority to those they expect to be measured by (the short-term goals). They either limit themselves to lip-service on long-term goals (typically in management meetings or seminars) or deal with them too briefly or superficially (more often out of ignorance of what is required than any intent to mislead).

For all the pitfalls that beset its path, development is constantly occurring. Our problem is that we need more than what seems to occur despite the pitfalls. Some organizations attract, hold, and develop capable managers without being overly concerned with courses, seminars, audiovisual materials, and the like. Whether by design or luck, they have managed to create an environment in which good people can grow.

In itself this is no reason for curtailing formal management development programs. But the ultimate yield from our investment in such programs depends much less on their content than on what the company's own style of management permits its managers to practice. To shop around for the "right" course or the "right" consultant is futile if what is taught cannot be effectively applied to, and reinforced on, the job.

In the end, life itself is our most potent teacher. If it is organized so as to be constrained, repetitive, and safe, it will teach us to ignore opportunities and shun the unknown. If it is organized so as to be challenging and risky, it will teach us to adapt to change and to evaluate the potential payoff in risk. The way in which an organization manages itself today is, willy-nilly, the classroom in which its next generation of managers will acquire both the vision and the blind spots with which they will meet the future.

Chapter 7
Absenteeism and Turnover

Surely the oldest and most enduring problem of management is the worker who does not come to work. Despite this antiquity, absenteeism and its more permanent counterpart, turnover, are not well understood. Consequently they are often mismanaged. They have little in common, other than their most superficial symptom—someone's unavailability for work. Yet that is so fundamental a consideration that it is logical to examine them together.

The contrast between absenteeism and turnover could hardly be sharper.

—Absenteeism results in only temporary unavailability. It is characteristic of lower-paid occupations. It is typically dealt with (if at all) by threats of dismissal. Its effects on productivity are usually underestimated.

—Turnover results in permanent unavailability. It is characteristic of higher-paid occupations. It is typically dealt with (if at all) by financial blandishments or promises thereof. Its effects on productivity are usually overestimated.

As is typical with ill-understood phenomena, the causes of absenteeism and turnover are usually misdiagnosed or grossly oversimplified. In the past, absenteeism was viewed as a sort of moral failing. More recently it has been viewed as a symptom of the decline of the work ethic or a result of government pressure to employ groups whose work ethic is presumed to be relatively less developed—principally blacks and women. Turnover used to be regarded as denoting an unseemly lack of the loyalty due one's employer. More recently it has been thought to reflect the machinations of recruiters or of companies willing to buy the talent they cannot grow.

Leaving morals and loyalty aside (as proper subjects for theologians, not consultants) there are some grains of truth in all of these explanations—but only grains.

—Absenteeism has increased chiefly in low-skilled, repetitive jobs, which also happens to be where the bulk of minority employment has occurred. Absentee rates of minorities in higher-skilled jobs tend to approximate those of nonminorities. Thus the type of job is a likelier cause of absenteeism than the type of people doing it or their ethics. (This line of evidence does not exclude the possibility that certain identifiable groups have, at least at present, more of a tendency to absenteeism than others. It does exclude the possibility that such a tendency, if it exists, is the sole, simple, or major cause of rising absenteeism.)

—Most studies of turnover indicate that pay differentials provide the occasion, not the cause, for leaving. Pay differences provide a convenient excuse for doing what one has already determined to do for other reasons. Those "other" reasons—the real reasons rather than the rationalizations—are more likely to lie in inadequate opportunities for development or advancement. Once again, the evidence points to the job.

Perhaps, then, we can add two other similarities between absenteeism and turnover to our initial one. Management tends to blame them both on forces beyond its control, but the evidence points to factors that are very much under management's control.

With both absenteeism and turnover, we can differentiate general causes affecting large numbers of individuals, and therefore addressable by policies, from individual causes that vary from person to person and are therefore best addressed by supervisors on a case-by-case basis. For the balance of this chapter we will deal separately with each problem, first on a general and then on a specific level.

Absenteeism: Costs

Most estimates of the cost of absenteeism confine themselves to counting days lost. In those companies where absentees are not penalized by loss of pay, total days lost can be multiplied by the average wage rate to obtain wages paid for work not done. This could be a considerable figure in itself. In companies that operate on low profit margins, wages paid for work not done can exceed profits. However, the wage cost of absenteeism is only a small fraction of its true total cost. This can best be gauged by considering the problem faced by a supervisor when one subordinate fails to show up for work for one day. Basically, the supervisor must choose among three alternatives.

—The easiest course of action is to do nothing and simply let the employee's work wait. Of course, this confronts the returning employee with two days of work or puts the person a day behind schedule. In an effort to catch up, the employee will tend to work faster, cut corners, and take short-cuts. As a result, the quality of work done during this catch-up phase is likely to be lower than normal. Further, if the work of other employees is affected by the timeliness with which the work of the absentee is done, they will also be inconvenienced or delayed.

—Rather than endure delays, the supervisor may distribute the absentee's work among the employees who did come to work. For example, if the absentee is one of ten employees in a department, the supervisor could distribute about an 11 percent additional workload to each of the nine present employees, and in all probability the department could handle it without falling behind. But the overload will inevitably be handled with greater fatigue, and probably greater annoyance, than the employees' own work. As a result it is not likely to be handled with the same care as regularly scheduled work. Thus, while schedules may not suffer under this alternative, quality will probably decline.

—The third alternative is to find a substitute for the absent employee. This alternative is inescapable if the work of the employees in the department is linked—as is the case, for example, in an assembly line or similar operation. But finding a suitable substitute and bringing that person to the right place takes time. A fifteen or twenty minute delay is not at all unusual, even in organizations which anticipate such problems and maintain labor pools to replace absentees. Thus, while merely waiting for a substitute to arrive, about 3 or 4 percent of the scheduled productive time of the employees who are present is irretrievably lost. The substitute is also unlikely to be as proficient at the job as the absentee. Further, the person knows perfectly well that this particular assignment, supervisor, or group of fellow-workers may never be seen again. For their part, the other workers in the department are likely to regard the substitute as an outsider. Thus the motivational forces playing on the substitute are likely to be negative, with the result that neither the quality nor the quantity of output matches that of the absentee.

The impact that absenteeism has on quality, delivery, and the efficiency with which equipment and employee time are used greatly exceeds the mere cost of paying absentees for days when they don't come to work. But the accountant usually posts these costs to where they are detected (such as quality) rather than to where they are caused (in this case, absenteeism). Thus management tends to underestimate the absentee problem and may be content to deal with it in superficial ways, such as posters on bulletin boards or brochures in pay envelopes.

The most serious costs of absenteeism are reduction in quality, inefficient use of fixed and human assets, and disruption of schedules. All of these losses are compounded when an absence is unexpected. For this reason, some companies offer a "bonus" of time off (in addition to vacations and holidays) for workers who maintain perfect attendance records, provided the free time is scheduled in advance. (A typical formula would be one-half day of free time for four consecutive weeks of perfect attendance—in effect, about six extra days per year.) The advantage of the plan is that scheduled absences are far less disruptive than unscheduled ones. The disadvantages are the granting of what amounts to about 2 percent loss of scheduled work time with no guarantee of an offsetting increase in overall productivity, plus the fact that the plan deals with symptoms rather than causes. Nevertheless, some harried personnel managers have found this a worthwhile trade-off.

Absenteeism: General Causes

Most policies that attempt to deal with absenteeism are based on the assumption that it results from a lack of self-discipline, or a lack of understanding of the importance of regular job attendance. They therefore try to supply what is lacking. To rectify the supposed shortage of discipline, management resorts to warnings, suspensions without pay, and dismissal. To deal with the lack of understanding, management resorts to various appeals, mostly of the published or posted (and therefore impersonal) variety. On the whole, these policies have a somewhat spotty record. Sometimes they are effective, at least to a degree and under certain circumstances; and sometimes they are ineffective. At the present state of our knowledge about this oldest of management problems, generalizations about policies are difficult.

The following cases are not presented as models of sophisticated absentee control. They are presented because they are real and because they demonstrate a variety of methods and a variety of results. They are not necessarily representative of industry as a whole, although many of their features are quite common. All three represent attempts to deal with widespread absenteeism involving many individuals by means of policies applicable to groups. In other words, they are for the most part "shotgun" approaches, designed to deal with large segments of large problems. Where it is used, counseling is patterned rather than individualized. The approaches make minimal demands on the supervisors of absentees. Therefore, their ultimate effectiveness depends not so much on the skill with which they are executed as on the appropriateness of their design to the specific group with which they are used.

Company W had several large manufacturing facilities, all of which operated around the clock on a three-shift basis. Absenteeism was a chronic, nagging problem. Management found it necessary to employ a pool of so-called "miscellaneous workers" whose function was to substitute for absentees. In effect the company hired 110 people for every 100 jobs, paying what amounted to a 10 percent premium to ensure against excessive disruption.

The plan usually met management's main objective, which was the prevention of total shutdowns of vital equipment or entire departments. On the other hand, it did nothing to reduce absenteeism and may even have encouraged it. Any employee who wanted to take a day off was not constrained by fears that the company, or fellow employees, would be unduly discomfited. For this reason, management found it necessary to supplement its policy with a program of graded discipline, ranging from verbal warnings to formal written warnings, to disciplinary suspensions, and finally to separation. This program was relatively lenient, since it had to be negotiated with the union. As a result, the great majority of days lost did not come within the purview of the policy, especially in its more severe aspects. Daily absentee rates tended to hover just below 10 percent.

These conditions persisted for several years. The direct labor cost in manufacturing was quite high, partly because of overmanning and partly because of the disruptions that absenteeism tended to create. Nevertheless, continued heavy demand for the company's products made this relatively inefficient system reasonably profitable. But when a particularly severe recession struck, a sharp reduction in demand led to a sudden overload of the company's products in wholesalers' warehouses. As a result, management ordered production cutbacks, which included laying off about two hundred of the production workers with the least seniority. With less production needed, management planned to operate fewer of its production lines and therefore expected to need fewer workers.

This was the first layoff in many years, and its effect on the employees was remarkable. Absentee rates suddenly dropped to about 3 percent. This drop was too great to be accounted for by the relative handful of employees whose absentee records had put them in danger of dismissal. Instead, the shock of the layoff seemed to imbue those employees who had previously been inclined to casual or sporadic absenteeism with a new appreciation of the importance of regular attendance. The layoff had communicated what posters and pamphlets had not.

Ironically, the reduction of the absentee rate more than offset the effect of the layoff. Employees were reporting to work in record numbers, and to keep them occupied, management assigned them to equipment that had been scheduled for shutdown. Thus, contrary to plans, production actually rose while demand declined. Management then found itself in the unusual position of having to order a further layoff— caused by the inconvenient spurt of motivation rather than by the sagging economy. As the recession was gradually relieved, absenteeism tended to drift back toward its previous levels.

For many years, Company K, which was nonunion, had followed a policy designed to discourage casual absenteeism. It consisted of not paying an employee for any one-day absence or for the first several consecutive days. The policy seemed to work well enough, and absenteeism held at around 3 percent for several years.

Management then undertook a searching review of its employee relations policies, some of which were very old, in order to determine whether they were consistent with a desire to manage in a modern, sophisticated way. In particular, management was impressed with the need for trust, mutual confidence, and open relationships. In this context, the absentee policy seemed both old-fashioned and coercive. After a careful review, management announced that the policy would be changed. Henceforth, no pay would be withheld for any absence.

Management had made an emphatic demonstration of its modernity and its trust in the self-discipline of its employees. Absenteeism, however, promptly doubled to about 6 percent. For a time, a deeply embarrassed management seemed to be caught in the dilemma of either retracting its policy and exposing its "modernity" as a sham, or living with the higher absentee rate and branding its employees as exploiters of a liberal policy.

The problem was addressed simultaneously by several actions. This tendency to procedural overkill is common enough in companies that want to extricate themselves quickly from an embarrassment. From the standpoint of scientists who would like to be able to identify each cause with its effect, this type of reaction is most inconvenient. There is no way to determine which of the actions helped to produce the ultimate effect and to what extent each worked.

In this case, two actions seemed to be more important than the rest. One was what might be called a public relations campaign. The other was a program of training supervisors to deal with individual absentees.

Company K had a profit-sharing plan which annually provided a substantial share of most employees' total income. Absenteeism, of course, was hurting profits and would tend to reduce the fund available for distribution to all plan members. The company's internal publication stressed this fact, pointing out that employees who stayed away from work unnecessarily were not only reducing their own income but that of their colleagues as well. Partly by making obvious a point which had evidently escaped certain employees, partly through subtle pressures that were no doubt exerted by employees on those of their fellows whom they suspected of abusing the absence privilege, this campaign probably helped to reduce the problem.

The training program for supervisors was designed to enable them to acquaint absentees with the consequences of their absence. Supervisors were taught to *avoid* questioning the reasons given for an absence. (Although such questions are often put to returning absentees, the answers are seldom enlightening. Further, having to answer the question is more likely to make employees resentful and defensive than to motivate them to improve their absence record.) Instead the supervisors in Company K were trained to point out the specific delays, inconveniences, overloads, and other problems that the absence caused. The supervisors then asked the employee to try to come to work regularly and to stay away only if necessary.

The combination of actions was effective, over a period of about six months, in gradually restoring the absence rate to its original level. In retrospect, it is clear that the introduction of the new policy without adequate explanation of its purposes had resulted in a binge of mostly experimental absenteeism. Some additional absences were probably quite legitimate, in that some employees who felt too ill to work may have felt constrained, under the old policy, to come to work anyway. But the great majority of the increase was simply due to reveling in a new privilege without appreciating its cost or purpose.

Company M, which was unionized, had suffered from an extraordinarily high absence rate (up to 13 percent) at one of its plants for quite some time. Absenteeism at this level can be extremely disruptive, sometimes resulting in the unscheduled shutdowns of entire departments. Almost in desperation, the company sought the cooperation of the union.

As the problem was initially defined by both parties, there seemed to be very little room for agreement. Management wanted the right to fire absentees sooner—that is, with fewer warnings and after fewer absences —than before. For its part, the union was primarily interested in protecting jobs, not eliminating them. Both parties realized that absenteeism simply *had* to be reduced or the plant might have to be shut down, with the consequent loss of all jobs.

Eventually it became clear to both parties that firing was not the central issue. Firing was merely a device, and not necessarily the only or most effective one, for reducing absenteeism—the central issue. Once this roadblock was surmounted, the negotiators moved swiftly to design a four-part program:

1. Management agreed that no one would be fired for absenteeism, regardless of how many absences had occurred.

2. The union agreed that once a certain level of absence was reached by any employee (defined as exceeding the plant average during any forty consecutive days) the employee would be subject to compulsory counseling. From that point, and for as long as his absence record exceeded the plant average for the preceding forty days, he would be subject to automatic suspension without pay for each further absence, beginning with a half day suspension for the first such absence. A unique feature of this plan was that the length of *each* subsequent suspension *doubled* (one day, two days, four days).

In other words, the suspensions rapidly became Draconian, and the unrepentant absentee soon found the cost of further absenteeism to be excessive. Many quit, despairing of ever getting their absence records down to unpunished levels. In order to provide some hope of redemption for such people, the union demanded (and management agreed) to the third part of this four-part approach.

3. Anyone whose absence record exposed him to suspensions could, by keeping his absence record at or below the plant average for forty consecutive days, wipe the slate clean. That is, his previous absences would no longer be held against him.

4. The last element was counseling, which was provided intensively on an individual basis by the personnel department. Anyone exposed to

suspension saw a great deal of the personnel department and heard a great deal about the consequences of absenteeism for his department and on his paycheck. These sessions got a mixed reception; some found them enlightening and others found them boring. But the effect in either case was the same. Whether it was due to a more mature understanding of the consequences of their behavior, or a simple desire to win release from listening to compulsory sermons, most counseled employees did get their absence rates down to an acceptable level.

Over a four-year period, the combined effect of these programs was a gradual reduction in the average rate of absenteeism for the entire plant from an excessive and dangerous level at 13 percent to a rate that compares quite favorably with that of most industrial plants—3 to 4 percent. Further, this greatly reduced rate has been sustained (at this writing) for two consecutive years. Although some of the more chronic absentees have found it expedient to resign rather than cope with escalating suspensions, no one has been fired for absenteeism; and several of the worst offenders have redeemed themselves by learning to control what was evidently just a very bad habit.

Company M's approach employed a combination of constructive and coercive measures—combining the carrot (forgiveness, counseling, and no firings) with the stick (doubling the length of each consecutive suspension). *Company W's* approach to absentee control can be characterized as "no carrot and a weak stick"—that is, it had no discernible effect on absenteeism except when severe economic conditions reminded employees of the value of a job. *Company K's* approach was virtually all "carrot," although it probably did induce a certain amount of discreet "stick waving" in the form of peer pressure by the employees themselves.

Absenteeism: Specific Causes

First-level supervisors can do a great deal to bring absenteeism down to manageable proportions. In fact, they can probably do more to limit absenteeism than anyone else in management, including executives who negotiate labor contracts and set company policies. To do this supervisors must first diagnose the particular type of absenteeism they are dealing with, then select an appropriate strategy for reducing it, and finally (perhaps most important of all) persist in the use of that strategy until it either shows results or becomes clearly futile.

Although absenteeism has a common effect—the unavailability of an employee to do assigned work—it has many causes. Five of the most common types of absenteeism are considered here. While it is rare to encounter employees who fit these types exactly, most absentees will fit one of the patterns at least reasonably well.

Chronic absentees have developed the habit of staying away from work because of relatively minor discomforts or inconveniences that most people would simply take in stride. They are not malingerers; in their own minds, the difficulties really are too much to cope with. In effect, they have a bad habit that substantially diminishes their availability for work. (The quality of their work, when they are present, may be quite good.) Chronic absentees can usually be distinguished by three signs: (1) they consistently account for more days lost than other people in the department, (2) they have very little tolerance for pressure or frustration, and (3) this pattern has continued for a long time.

Escapist absentees are those whose interest in their job is so low that other interests—especially hobbies and other enjoyable pursuits—compete effectively with the job for their time. Hunting, fishing, golf, or attending entertainment events are common examples of what escapist absentees do when absent. In these individuals the motivation for work is largely economic, and the work itself has little, if any, inherent attraction. From time to time, escapist absentees find that they need a respite, and they take time from work to do whatever they find more attractive. Basically, they are trying to extricate themselves, at least temporarily, from a situation they dislike but cannot afford to leave permanently.

This type of absenteeism has been increasing in recent years. Job boredom is probably no more common that it ever was; but today's workers (especially the younger ones) are less concerned about the prospect of losing a job, or of displeasing a superior, than previous generations were. In some companies, escapist absenteeism is a major cause of person/days lost—especially where younger workers are a disproportionately large part of the total work force and where they tend to be assigned to repetitive jobs. The distinguishing marks of escapist absenteeism are: (1) it occurs sporadically, a day here and a day there rather than several consecutive days, (2) it tends to fall just before or just after a weekend or a holiday, and (3) almost always the absentees feel underutilized in their job.

Immature absentees are not necessarily young, although this is the leading kind of absenteeism among younger workers. The "immaturity" refers to ideas and attitudes, not ages. Immature absentees are people who do not take their work seriously, who feel that absenteeism is a sort of "fringe benefit" to which they are entitled, and who are likely to be influenced in their own absence habits by what they see other workers doing. For example, the introduction of escapist or chronic absentees into the work group is likely to cause immature persons' absenteeism to rise. They are people who regard someone else's absenteeism as an adequate excuse for their own.

This problem nearly always disappears as the individual grows older. But while it lasts it can cause severe disruption. It is particularly aggravating for supervisors whose departments normally include younger employees; no sooner is the problem corrected in one individual than another young worker (who may look upon the workplace as a sort of psychological extension of school) comes along to replace the first.

Abusive absentees are comparatively rare, but they are so difficult and so memorable that it sometimes seems there are more such people than really exist. Usually these are unhappy individuals who feel that other people are trying to take advantage of them, or that the only way to be assured fair treatment is to aggressively take whatever they feel is their due. This attitude can focus on any aspect of work, such as safety requirements or quality standards. When it focuses on absenteeism, the result is likely to be a series of "retaliations" for excused absences by others.

Abusive absentees are less interested in time off than in proving a point, which is that they will not tolerate what they regard as favoritism or unfair treatment. They usually make little attempt to disguise the reasons for their absence. In fact, they are likely to have a well-rehearsed speech, justifying their own behavior and denouncing the supervisor or the company, which they are all too eager to deliver. Obviously, abusive absentees are very trying to the supervisor's patience and very demanding of the supervisor's skill.

Finally there are *legitimate absentees*—those who are unable to work due to illness, or who must be absent for a reason which the company's rules recognize. Sooner or later, this includes virtually everyone. The identification of the legitimate absentee is easy; when absences are rare, they are probably legitimate. Of course, one can't be sure in every case, but the occasional absentee accounts for so small a proportion of total days lost that the supervisor is well advised to concentrate on those individuals (including the first four types) who account for the greater share.

The advantage a supervisor has over any bureaucratic procedure—the knowledge of each employee's behavior patterns—should be exploited to the hilt. Any absence control procedure that is likely to work is also likely to be time-consuming and somewhat onerous for supervisor and employee alike. Therefore the supervisor should concentrate on those employees—usually a relative handful—who account for the bulk of days lost to absenteeism and deal with occasional absentees only to the extent required by policy.

By focusing attention on the main offenders, the supervisor will not only get the greatest return for the effort but will also indirectly discourage increases in immature (or "conformist") absenteeism. With the more frequent absentees, the supervisor should attempt to determine whether their behavior approximates any of the above patterns. One seldom encounters a "pure case," but the majority of frequent absentees will come reasonably close to one of them. It is very important to note that no special training is needed to diagnose absence patterns. All the relevant evidence is directly before the supervisor's eyes, and no one else is in a better position to analyze and interpret that evidence.

One absence control technique that a supervisor can use is showing the absentee the specific consequences of each absence on the department and on fellow employees. This is especially useful with chronic absentees, who often have a "need to be needed" but manage to convince themselves that they are not, and thus fail to recognize how their presence is, in fact, important to their colleagues. The supervisor points out the specific disruptions, delays, inconveniences, and frustrations that the absence caused. Perhaps these things should be obvious, but the simple truth of the matter is that people whose behavior is objectionable to others usually manage to remain oblivious of the problems they are causing; and unless they are told, they will remain oblivious.

This type of feedback about one's own behavior is always likely to be unwelcome, sometimes likely to be rejected, and frequently likely to be forgotten. For these reasons, the treatment has to be used persistently if it is to have a significant effect. It is a way of arousing guilt and putting it into conflict with the temptation to stay away from work. Virtually no one likes to feel guilty or arouse guilt in others, which is why this procedure is onerous—and also why it works.

Basically, chronic absentees are those who have not become adult in the sense of anticipating, and accepting responsibility for, the consequences of their own actions. Having those consequences inexorably called to their attention is likely to seem, in their eyes, like a form of punishment. For a while, at least, after each such exposure, they are likely to be motivated to avoid another one—with the result that at least some occasions when they would ordinarily have stayed away from the job will be converted to working days.

A second technique is to show the effects of absenteeism on the absentees themselves. This is especially useful with the escapist type of absentee, where the basic problem is a mismatch between the individual's interests or abilities and the content of the job—and where the only permanent cure is transfer or promotion to a more appropriate assignment. Once again, the absentee tends to be oblivious to the consequences of the absenteeism—in this case, to the fact that it greatly decreases the likelihood that a cure can be effected. It makes the absentee an unattractive candidate for transfer or promotion—so effectively, in fact, that these problems are all too seldom cured, and many an escapist absentee eventually becomes a statistic in a turnover report.

With the escapist absentee, the supervisor is engaged in a holding action. The objective is to hold absenteeism down long enough to be able to effect a transfer or, failing that, to at least prolong the individual's usefulness. Making such people aware that their reaction to the basic problem is, in effect, blocking any permanent solution to it, offers some hope of enlisting their self-control in the battle against their tendency to flee from the job.

A third technique, aimed particularly at immature absentees is to appeal to their desire to be thought of and treated as adults. This calls for pointing out things they probably "know" in an intellectual sense but have not yet assimilated into their behavior: that absences are a provision for emergencies rather than a fringe benefit; that absences motivated by the thrill of getting away with a rule violation are childish and unworthy of an adult; that absences taken because other people have been absent are irresponsible mimicry; that the job exists because it needs to be done, and it therefore has an importance to the company and its customers that transcends the momentary interests and impulses that distract—but need not motivate—us all.

In this approach, the supervisor is trying to accelerate the employees' process of growing up by pointing out things they would probably discover for themselves sooner or later. Of course, the object is to have the truisms discovered sooner rather than later. Unfortunately, pointing out such things shades over all too readily into patronization and condescension; hence the supervisor who does it must be at some pains to preserve the employees' dignity by avoiding even a semblance of scorn or sarcasm.

In most cases, threats are not an effective method of absence control. They address symptoms rather than causes and are likely to motivate some kind of hidden retaliation (usually by damaging the company's products or services, which can be treated as symbols of its management). However, there is one exception; abusive absentees are seldom amenable to any of the positive approaches cited above. The only effective way to deal with them is to state the limits of acceptable behavior (whether absenteeism or anything else) firmly and clearly and indicate precisely what punishments will be meted out for each level of offense. Further, the threats must be promises of retribution rather then mere warnings, and the retribution must be swift and sure. These cases are rare, and, therefore, so is the applicability of threats to absenteeism.

Supervisory approaches to absence control are time-consuming—all the more so because they require frequent repetition. Further, there isn't a panacea among them; none work always, or perfectly, or permanently. Their principal merit is that they are more effective than any other techniques available to management; and the trade-off is worth it. If these techniques can cut down the disruption, reduced quality, and inefficient use of resources caused by absenteeism, then the time, the awkwardness, and the risk of offending are all clearly worthwhile.

Turnover: Cost

The cost of turnover is well known and can be summarized briefly. It creates a need for replacement, which costs money. In large companies, full-time staffs must be retained to recruit, select, hire, and train replacements, even when the company is not actually growing. Productivity may suffer during the interval between the departure of an experienced employee and the attainment of full competence by the replacement.

If turnover is concentrated among younger employees (as it usually is), the effect is to deny the company a seasoned, thoroughly mature work force. If turnover includes employees who are highly regarded for their potential (as it often does), the effect is to prevent the company, in the future, from adhering to a policy of promotion from within.

If the turnover is among university graduates who are replaced by more recent graduates, the effect is often to induce salary compression by offering higher starting salaries to the most recent graduates than were offered to previous graduates. If the turnover is among employees who have contact with customers, relations with the customers may suffer.

Small wonder that defectors are personnel managers' perennial headache. After all, these managers are charged with keeping the company adequately staffed, and defectors simply undo their work. During periods of high turnover, personnel managers are likely to feel as if they were trying to shovel back the tide. Not a few of them regard economic recessions, when job opportunities dry up and turnover naturally declines, as a well-earned respite!

Turnover: Benefits

But there are also advantages to turnover. The most obvious is simply the opportunity to bring new talent, ideas, and techniques into the company. Sometimes people who make exceptional contributions to a company join it to fill a vacancy created by turnover. But turnover also has subtler advantages, which are more likely to occur than the fortuitous hiring of a genius.

For example, turnover is probably the most common (and most practical) solution to the ubiquitous problems of dead-end jobs and dull work. These are typically high turnover situations, and the sad truth is that very often nothing can be done to make them more attractive. Job enrichment (altering a job to make its content more stimulating to the incumbent) obviously can "work" only when it is feasible to use it; and it frequently isn't.

Employees who defect from dead-end or dull jobs usually spare their company a much more serious and intractable problem than the minor one caused by leaving. The longer they stay the greater the likelihood that they will eventually become utterly demotivated, embittered, and either inattentive or actively hostile to their work. Most people have a certain tolerance level for tedium, and once that level is passed (and no suitable new opportunity is available), it is best to accept their departure gracefully. As the following case shows, the cost of reducing such natural turnover sometimes exceeds the benefits— and by a wide margin.

A food company had local administrative offices in a number of key cities for the purpose of coordinating shipments to customers in the area, billing them, and receiving payments. Most of the jobs in these offices were clerical in nature and ranged in complexity from routine typing and filing to fairly complicated coordination of shipping schedules. It had been traditional for women to handle most of the work. Some clever secretaries had proven that they could learn to coordinate shipments with little difficulty. Also, becoming a coordinator represented a logical job progression for them.

During a particularly hectic period when sales of certain products normally peaked, two incidents occurred in which important customers complained of delays and incorrect shipments. When the newly-appointed manager of this group investigated, he found that both cases were related to unexpected resignations of female shipping coordinators. Both women had left for normal reasons—one to be married, the other to accompany her husband to another city to which he had been transferred. Both women had evidently given comparatively short notice, and a mild administrative chaos ensued until suitable replacements could be found and trained. After the second of these incidents, the manager decided that such confusion must not be allowed to happen again, and he developed a plan to prevent it.

He reasoned that a high turnover rate among young female employees was unavoidable. Therefore, his basic strategy was to decrease his reliance on them. He did this by increasing the proportion of new male employees whenever expansion or attrition created a hiring opportunity; he also moved men into shipping coordinator jobs whenever possible. Since the normal turnover rate among women was about four times that of men, within a few years there were virtually no women left in the coordinator jobs. The proportion of female employees, which previously had been a heavy majority, dropped to about 40 percent, and they were mostly typists and secretaries. The manager had solved *what he thought* was his problem.

Although shipping coordination was a highly important job from the company's standpoint, most of the men found that dealing with great masses of small details day after day was less than stimulating. Furthermore, shipping coordination in a local administrative office was a dead-end job, in the sense that it did not prepare one for available higher responsibilities. Opportunities for promotion into management in these offices were rather limited anyway.

Further, there were many men in these offices who had not yet advanced to shipping coordinator, because the hiring of larger proportions of men than women had continued even after most shipping coordinator jobs had been filled by men. These other men were employed in even duller work as record clerks or as accounting machine operators.

What the manager had really accomplished, after a few years, was to accumulate a large number of increasingly frustrated male employees who felt trapped, unable to progress, and taken for granted. Turnover among men, especially the clerks and machine operators, began to rise until it approached the normal rate for women.

There are also financial advantages to turnover, and while these are indirect, they are not inconsiderable. Turnover minimizes the number of employees whose wages and salaries rise beyond the midpoint of their pay range. The effect is a significant downward leverage on actual payroll costs, in most cases without any significant loss of productivity. This is because the productivity gain that comes with increased experience occurs, in most jobs, in the first few months or years after initial training —that is, while the individual's pay is still below the midpoint.

In jobs where individual productivity does not increase significantly beyond a certain experience level, pay increases beyond that point (regardless of what they are called) are merely rewards for not having quit. On the other hand, with turnover holding average experience levels down, pay is more closely tied to accomplishment; and whatever motivational effect derives from the prospect of several future pay increases operates with maximum effect on a large number of employees.

Turnover also affects the cost of funding pensions. The sum set aside for this purpose is based on actuarial estimates of the number of today's employees who will actually qualify for a pension in terms of full or partial vesting, both of which depend, of course, on how many stay and how many leave. It is impossible to say *which* individuals will stay, but it is possible to guess with remarkable accuracy *how many* will stay. Therefore, funds are set aside toward the ultimate pension of each employee so long as he or she remains an employee. When anyone leaves without having qualified for vesting, the funds set aside for this pension are retained and commingled with the funds set aside for those who have not left.

Therefore, the higher the turnover rate before vesting, the less the amount of funding *per employee* needed to achieve the necessary total funding. In effect, both the company and the employees who do not leave benefit at the expense of those who do leave. (To the extent that pensions become "portable," this advantage can be nullified.)

Beyond financial matters, turnover affects such important intangibles as a company's employment image. This is the set of beliefs and impressions held about a company by its prospective employees. A favorable image attracts a broad range of applicants and enables the company to be more selective than would normally be possible. The quality of its new employees should therefore surpass that of companies which are not considered attractive. It might seem that a high turnover rate would make applicants suspicious that something must be wrong. Actually, quite the opposite is often true.

Some companies acquire reputations for excellent training, so that a few years of employment become the résumé equivalent of an MBA, or of apprenticeship under a master craftsman, should one decide to return to the job market. Precisely because their experience has made them eminently marketable, many employees in such companies do exactly that. Those companies get high turnover rates. They also train, at their own expense, managers and technicians for other companies. On the surface such companies appear unfortunate.

But look beneath the surface. Because of their reputation for training, these companies attract the more ambitious job-seekers, and they can choose among them more selectively than can less sought-after companies. They are able to observe this select group in action as its members sort themselves out according to performance, and they can decide which few are the "cream of the cream." These few star performers need not be lost because, once identified, especially generous arrangements can be made for them. As for the rest, should they decide to leave, the company will suffer no lasting loss. They will usually have more than paid their own way, and their departure both stimulates and makes possible a continuing flow of young, eager, highly motivated replacements. In fact, one could argue that something may be wrong with a company that suffers too little turnover during an economic boom. Why are its employees not attractive to other employers?

Finally, turnover serves a desirable economic function. It transfers labor from where it is no longer needed to where it is wanted now. It matches supply to demand. If it were allowed to operate freely, turnover would greatly reduce the number of workers who are trapped in jobs they do not want, in companies which do not want them. On the employees' side, the gain in security and job satisfaction (and possibly even earning power) would be substantial. On the employer's side, overhead costs would decline while productivity improved.

The trouble, of course, is that our whole system of employment, compensation, and pensions is designed to discourage turnover. However, the system functions imperfectly; it "leaks." By studying the characteristics of those whom the system is not restraining now, we can make some educated guesses about turnover trends.

Turnover: General Causes

Broadly speaking, two definable demographic groups are more susceptible to voluntary turnover than any other groups: young people of all kinds (say, age twenty-five or less) and better-educated men in the thirty-five to forty-five age range. The first (younger) group includes both sexes and all levels of education; the second is much more narrowly defined.

In the younger group, turnover is largely caused by youth itself: impatience, limited tolerance for frustration, curiosity, lack of binding commitments, uncertainty as to what one really wants to do—and the fact that young people are often given the least desirable assignments. The problem is usually self-curing. Casual or impulsive turnover is rarely seen after the mid-twenties. (In fact, one simple way to bring down turnover rates—if that is what you really want—is to maximize hiring in the thirty and older age group.)

Youthful turnover is an old, established characteristic of the labor force. "Middle-aged" turnover, on the other hand, is comparatively new. Or rather, it is a new solution to an old problem: the loss of career options as one gets older and the increasing predictability of how one's career will end if nothing is done to redirect it. Thus there is an increasing tendency by university graduates in this age group to opt out of the organizations in which they have spent the bulk of their careers. Some go to higher positions in smaller firms, some to self-employment; still others change careers altogether, "starting all over again," as it were. Instead of merely tolerating mid-career frustrations, this group shows an increasing tendency to extricate itself from them.

Youthful turnover will probably remain at about its present levels, waxing when unemployment is low and waning when it is high. To the extent that younger workers of the future will enter the labor force at an older age, due to prolonged education, the waxing will probably be more pronounced. Mid-career turnover, on the other hand, will almost certainly rise, since the thirty-five to forty-five age group of the future will have a higher percentage of university graduates than today's. Also, many of the great "growth" companies of the 1960s and 1970s are maturing; they are past the point of inflection on their growth curves. Promotional opportunities will dry up, disappointing many an ambitious middle manager.

The prospect, then, is for more turnover. Economic recessions simply delay it, and it would take a full-scale depression to mark today's younger worker with the unswerving appreciation for steady work that characterizes the older generation. The leak in the system will get leakier.

But what about those who don't leave? They can be divided into three major groups: the "umbilical" types who probably would not wish to leave under any circumstances, save retirement; the currently contented types who may nonetheless become discontented in the future; and the reluctant types who would leave if they dared, or if someone would only offer them a suitable alternative. Of these, the reluctant types are of greatest interest here since any increase in turnover trends would probably sweep them—or at least some of them—into the ranks of the defectors. While reliable measurements are difficult, a reasonable rule of thumb is that for every actual defector there is at least one reluctant stayer (with similar demographic characteristics). There is, in other words, a substantial pool of prospective defectors to feed any increase in turnover.

Short-term turnover rates will no doubt continue to jiggle up and down, but the long-term trend is clearly up. The question facing management, therefore, is not how to reduce or contain turnover but how to manage it. How can rising turnover rates be put to good use?

Managing Turnover

The *number* of employees who defect is not nearly so important as *which* employees defect. To be blunt, most of us are replaceable.

But if most people are replaceable, a few are not, and the key to managing turnover lies in identifying those few defectors whose loss has left the company significantly and irredeemably weaker. The best way to do this is with an immediate "postmortem" performance appraisal. Quite a few companies use a procedure which more or less follows the outline given below; but for reasons that will presently become obvious, none of them advertise it.

The first step is to recognize that certain jobs are "critical sources," in that they normally provide candidates for higher-level jobs which are considered vital; performance in those jobs can significantly influence the company as a whole. Whenever anyone resigns from a critical source job, someone is assigned to interview all of the person's former supervisors and their superiors. (The personnel records jacket is usually useless for this purpose.) Or if it is convenient, the past and present supervisors may meet. The purpose is to recall and record what the defector did—not how anyone felt about or rated the person but what he or she actually *did*.

More specifically, the focus is on what was noteworthy—either remarkably good or remarkably bad. This is not an easy exercise, since most of us like to think about each other in general rather than specific terms. But if the group persists, what emerges are the highlights of what the defector did for, or to, the company. For the purposes of the judgment that must now be made, *nothing else matters.*

A succinct statement of the defector's principal actions is placed before former superiors, and they now sit as a jury to assess the magnitude of the loss created by the departure. They have to rate it in one of three categories:

—*Replaceable.* This is by far the most common category. Sentiment aside, it recognizes that no lasting, significant damage has been done.

—*Unclear.* This category is used when the evidence is equivocal, or insufficient, or when the group cannot agree.

—*Irreplaceable.* The group is unanimous, or nearly unanimous, in agreeing that the performance of the defector gave clear evidence of potential for effective performance in jobs at the vital level. This is the only kind of loss to which the company should *not* resign itself.

Trying to talk the "irreplaceable" defector out of leaving is usually inadvisable. The temptation to sample the outside world will probably recur, so persuasion is likely to do no more than defer the inevitable. Also, it is unwise to give anyone the impression that the way to win sizable, unscheduled salary increases is to announce one's intention to leave. Rather than stopping the departure of such a defector, the strategy is to re-recruit the person in the future.

The rest is mechanical. Someone in management is given the responsibility for maintaining loose, informal, but reasonably frequent contact with the defector. An occasional lunch, party, or golf date will suffice. No attempt is made to sell the person on returning. Instead someone simply keeps track of the defector's progress in, and satisfaction with, the new company.

In a typical situation, if a man's progress is slow, the old company must assess whether it has overestimated him, or his new company presents tougher obstacles than it did, or whether the new company is simply frustrating him. If he progresses well, that confirms the old company's judgment and increases its interest. If he is satisfied, it can only bide its time. (The only way it can "dissatisfy" him is exorbitantly expensive.) If he becomes dissatisfied himself, his former company will want to be aware of it on a timely basis so it can reassess its needs and decide whether to invite him to return under conditions in which he will feel most welcome. However, should such an invitation be issued, the previous employer could expect to encounter an extraordinarily delicate problem—one that is, in fact, the principal obstacle to using this method. That is the reaction of loyal employees who may feel that defectors are better rewarded than they are and that "the best way to get ahead in this company is to leave it."

Loyalty is an emotionally charged issue, and it is important to ask precisely what is meant by the term. In most cases loyalty is defined by something the employee did not do (that is, he or she did not leave) rather than by any action taken, such as declining offers of employment elsewhere or investing time and effort in work "beyond the call of duty." When loyalty consists of exceptional effort, it should obviously be rewarded in some tangible way, but not necessarily by reserving a vital job. When it consists of declining opportunities to defect, the assumption must be that those opportunities were less attractive than continued service in one's present company. When loyalty consists merely in not having left, surely an adequate reward is continued employment. On analysis, the "loyalty" issue is not a substantial impediment to re-recruiting the exceptionally valuable defector.

For other, replaceable defectors, the key question is: *When* do they leave? That is, after how much service? Basically, we want to know whether, on average, we are recouping our training investment and whether jobs in which "experience counts" are staffed, on average, by sufficiently experienced employees. The minimum periods for establishing these points can be estimated well enough for our purposes by simply asking the largest feasible number of knowledgeable managers to discuss these questions and then pool their estimates.

In the event people are leaving too soon, our objective is not to stop the exodus but simply to slow it—that is, to increase the average length of employment. The standard prescription here has three parts.

—First, find out why people are leaving. Instead of "exit interviews" while they are still on the payroll, contact them four to six weeks after they have left—when they are likely to be both more objective and more voluble. Look for patterns, not individual problems. Concentrate on patterns that management can do something about—and then *do* that something.

—Second, make sure that wages or salaries are competitive. (With younger employees, spendable income is usually more important than fringe benefits. With older employees, including "mid-career defectors," the total compensation package has to be considered.)

—Third, try to increase nonfinancial satisfactions, especially by decreasing unnecessary controls on personal initiative and by adding planning and decision functions to the jobs most afflicted by turnover.

In the event people are not leaving too soon—that is, the company has realized a profit from its investment in them, and not too many jobs are held by relatively inexperienced people—we should view their departure with equanimity. If we are farsighted we should even view it with a certain relief. Probably the gracious thing to do would be to take them to dinner and wish them godspeed.

Chapter 8
Grievances

In the narrow context of a labor contract, grievances are union members' complaints that they have not been treated as the contract says they should be. More broadly, grievances are complaints of any sort: of unfairness, injury in some financial or psychological sense, or failure to keep a promise. Sooner or later, human nature and organizational life being what they are, virtually everyone is likely to be aggrieved.

Grievances have some of the characteristics of a fluid. If channels are not provided for them, they will cut their own. They can be dammed, but if so they will exert pressure against the weakest point, so the dam is always in danger of giving way. They can be condemned, ignored, or debated with—none of which will make them go away.

Grievances themselves are probably inevitable. However, it does not follow that their more destructive consequences are also inevitable. The most aggravated grievances are those which have been treated for too long as if they did not, and should not, exist. A wise management, far from ignoring or suppressing grievances, seeks them out. It tries to redress those that are redressable and to explain why the rest cannot be changed. Unfortunately, this is one of the many instances in which it is easier and more comfortable for management to be unwise—at least initially. As the following case illustrates, the penalty for unwisdom about grievances can be very severe indeed.

A company that made central heating and air conditioning equipment for large buildings also provided a repair and maintenance service for its products. The company's management had long felt that this service was costing more than necessary and that an adequate level of service could be provided at less cost. Eventually, one of the executives who had been most critical of the inefficiency of the service department was placed in charge of it; he was instructed to reduce its costs without significantly impairing the quality of the service.

Since the labor content of service work is very high, his main emphasis was on reducing manpower levels. He did this without layoffs, partly by not replacing all of the servicemen who left for normal reasons (such as retirement or accepting jobs with other companies) and partly by hiring new servicemen more slowly than the growth of new heating and air conditioning installations warranted.

The combined effect of these policies was to increase the average workload of individual servicemen. At the same time, the service director reduced the ratio of first-level supervisors to servicemen by creating new supervisory positions at a rate slower than the growth of the service organization as a whole.

These actions were successful in achieving the result he was seeking, which was a lower cost of operations without significantly impairing the quality of service itself—at least initially. Unfortunately, the effects of his actions were not confined to cost reduction. At first the men did not object to additional work, since they had spent a fair amount of their time in idleness under the former system. But they soon began to complain that they had insufficient time to properly diagnose the malfunctions of systems they were sent to repair. The sheer volume of repair compelled them to neglect preventive maintenance, which had the effect of increasing the number of equipment failures and raising the number of repair calls they had to make.

They complained that they could no longer take pride in their work because their repairs had to be hasty, and they began having the humiliating experience (for skilled mechanics) of being called back to repair again a unit they had just "fixed" a few hours previously. A general decline in morale set in, worsened by the fact that there were fewer promotional opportunities (due to the decreased ratio of supervisors to workers) and fewer opportunities to discuss their problems with their supervisors (for the same reason).

At about this point, reports began to reach the service director about grumbling and unrest among the men. He took the position that some degree of complaining was normal and inevitable, and he therefore saw no reason to take special notice of it. Somewhat later, one of his field managers—a loyal old veteran who was nearing retirement—asked to see him privately and confided that he was worried about the deterioration in the attitudes of the servicemen in his area. The service director became annoyed and told the field manager that he was overreacting to unjustified complaints from a few malcontents.

At a meeting of all field managers a few weeks later, the service director made a speech defending his cost reduction policies. He pointed out that they had been effective from a financial standpoint and claimed that all of the changes he had introduced had been necessary, and indeed overdue. He praised the field managers for their cooperation thus far and urged them to continue seeking ways to eliminate waste and inefficiency. His objective, he said, was "a lean, taut, highly efficient team."

During the general discussion period which followed his speech, two of the field managers (not including the one who had already visited his office) expressed apprehension about the sullen, almost angry attitudes they were beginning to see among the servicemen. They suggested that the men might not understand the reasons for the policies and that it might help if he would visit the field whenever possible to speak to them.

The service director had been working hard for several months. He was tired and irritable, not at his best. Normally a thoughtful, considerate man, he reacted with uncharacteristic roughness. Rising to his feet and interrupting the second field manager, he launched into what could only be described as a tirade. Any sensible person, he said, could see that his policies were fair and necessary. It was the duty of field managers to defend those policies to the men, not to repeat the illogical and unjustified complaints of a few loudmouths who did not know what they were talking about. "There is *no* morale problem!" he insisted. "There is *no* morale problem because there is no *reason* why there should be one!"

As a result of this memorable outburst, field managers concluded that further references to morale problems would be not only futile but possibly dangerous. Therefore, while the instances of complaints and bitterness that they encountered among the servicemen increased, they did not report them. When pressed by their men, they offered a variety of vague and lame explanations. In the meantime, the service director felt vindicated in his diagnosis that the complaints were trivial, since he heard no more about them. Consequently, he forgot about them.

It was not until almost a year later that he had any reason to recall the brief flurry of warnings he had received from his field managers. One day an organizer for a large labor union called on him at his office, claimed to have signed membership cards from more than half the servicemen, and demanded that the union be recognized as their exclusive bargaining agent. The service director was flabbergasted but had the presence of mind to petition instead for an election. However, the union won the election, and as a result of generous contracts and various work rules introduced over the next few years, the cost of providing maintenance service to customers rose far above its original levels.

Cost reduction campaigns in themselves do not necessarily produce cost-increasing behavioral reactions, as this one did. The reaction was entirely due to the mishandling of the accumulated grievances. By damming them up, which is what the service director unwittingly did when he denounced the attempts of his field managers to warn him of the complaints they had received, he virtually assured some kind of explosive response. In this case, the response negated all that he had accomplished.

The Psychology of Grievances: Employees

The dynamics of blocked grievances run something like this.

—In the first stage, a relative handful of employees—perhaps the more sensitive ones—take note of some condition they dislike. They may grumble a bit, especially if this is one in a long series of unwelcome experiences, but for the most part their reactions are subdued.

—In the second stage, they begin to recognize that their views are shared by others. The complaints are talked about more openly—usually in "safe" settings such as locker rooms, taverns, or parking lots. An "infectious" process begins, as the employees who are susceptible to the views of their more voluble colleagues begin to swing over to those views.

—In the third stage, the grievance is held, or supported, by a large enough proportion of the employees that most of the remainder are very quickly swung over, if only by the force of conformity.

—The fourth stage may continue for quite some time, depending on how effectively the expression of the grievance is blocked. A long, slow, "smoldering" process occurs, during which management's failure to respond to the grievance, rather than the grievance itself, becomes the principal issue. Management may come to be viewed as callous or arrogant.

—Whether the fifth stage is ever reached depends on the exasperation of the employees, on the apparent chances that management can be swayed, and perhaps more than anything else on the fortuitous presence of a "spark": some precipitating incident, usually trivial in itself, that is somehow symbolic to the employees of "the last straw." If that happens, the reaction can be explosive. It is not inevitable; but once the fourth stage is reached, it is always potential.

The specific issues that employees will complain about in the smoldering fourth stage or the explosive fifth stage are likely to be essentially the same as those they merely grumbled about in the first stage. Therefore the smoldering and the explosion are produced not by the issues themselves but by the length of time management has ignored them.

In the above case, field managers became aware of the problem in the second stage. Some may even have sensed it as early as the first stage. They reported the problem to their chief while the third stage was developing. Once the service director let loose his tirade, the fourth stage was inevitable. The spark that produced the fifth stage was a clever union organizer, who recognized that a group which hitherto had little interest in being organized had now become ripe. A ready-made issue was handed to him: the need for a protected grievance channel. Labor unions specialize in providing exactly that kind of channel, and this is no small reason for their success.

Unions did not create the issue of grievance channels. They merely exploited an issue that is inherent in any authority relationship between adults—an issue which most managements had not dealt with at all, at least until well after the advent of widespread unionization. The basic issue is power: the ability to force or constrain someone else's behavior. The question of how best to cope with power is one of the enduring dilemmas not only of organizations but of societies as well. It is the classical confrontation of the individual and the group.

The ultimate form of power wielded by an organization is the denial of employment (either through not hiring or through firing). But it is the mere possibility of firing, regardless of whether it is ever exercised or hinted at, that produces a coercive effect. Many employees who feel that their organization has violated its own rules, or simple fairness, with respect to themselves may feel constrained from seeking redress simply because they have far less to gain than they have to lose. Thus it is by no means rare for relatively trivial grievances to accumulate until, by their sheer number and age, they develop into sullen antagonisms. Attitudes of this kind can be found even in organizations that neither fire nor threaten firing. The agent that produces the antagonism is not fear of firing but fear of complaining. Failure to provide a safe channel for voicing complaints and seeking redress lies at the root of aggravated employee relations in many companies which, paradoxically, treat their employees well in all other respects.

There seem to be two main psychological mechanisms through which most people try to cope with the issue of organizational power. Some tend to regard the power exercised by management as benevolent, or at any rate legitimate. They do not question it and may even come to rely on it as a source of strength and guidance—much as a child might regard a parent. (Note, however, that this comparison is only descriptive; it does *not* imply a simple transfer of attitudes from parents to managers.) Other people are more wary about the potential abuse of organizational power, even if they perceive no current abuse. This group usually feels the need for some kind of check on management (a countervailing force, if you will) to restrain such abuses and to correct them if they occur despite restraint.

It is difficult to say which of these groups is larger. They are not strictly defined, and not enough is known to permit many generalizations about individual differences in reactions to organizational power. But it is clear that such differences exist, and they account for a large part of the variation in employee reactions to managerial styles. These differing individual predispositions are also probably the main cause of the disagreements between various managerial gurus as to whether "workers" want to be firmly or leniently led. It is patently absurd to generalize about *all* workers; and the "evidence" marshaled by either side to support the universality of its claim usually consists of little more than instances that happen to fit—which are not hard to find if one goes looking for them.

Pending a clearer delineation of this problem than the present state of behavioral science permits, the following tentative distinctions seem to have at least some validity.

—People who *accept* organizational power over themselves tend to be less educated, older, and less upwardly mobile (in the sense of improving income, social status, and financial independence). They also tend to have their origins in ethnic or religious groups and/or geographical regions in which traditional authority of all kinds is generally not questioned.

—People who *want restrictions* on organizational power tend to be more educated, younger, and more upwardly mobile. They also tend to originate in ethnic or religious groups and/or geographic regions in which authority often is questioned.

To the extent that these generalizations are valid, it appears that the social and economic changes of the past few decades are increasing the size of the second (power restricting) group in the population at large. This trend seems likely to continue for the foreseeable future. Thus the number of organizations in which it would be at least politic (and at most imperative) to provide adequate grievance channels may be safely estimated as both large and growing.

While we are now considering the need for checks on organizational power in the context of grievances, it is important to recognize that the same need has important effects on other aspects of organizational life as well. The whole problem of performance appraisal, which we will consider in the next chapter, is intimately bound up with the question of the organization's power over its members. Further, studies of motivation have shown a clear tendency for employees who have shared in the decision processes affecting them to implement those decisions with increased effort and cooperation. Finally, labor unions are best understood as countervailing forces against unbridled and distrusted management freedom. Thus grievances are only an instance, albeit a particularly important one, of a larger problem inherent in the relationship between individuals and any organization which, because they are economically dependent on it, wields power over them.

The Psychology of Grievances: Managers

Earlier in this chapter we noted that it is often easier and more comfortable for managers not to seek out or redress employee grievances. There are at least four common reasons for this reluctance, and the effective manager must learn to cope with all four.

—The most common reason for ignoring the question of grievances is a genuine belief that there are none, or at least none serious enough to worry about. This springs from a simple projection of management's intentions toward employees—which are usually benevolent and fair, to the extent that they are conscious at all—and from management's daily experience with employees—which is likely to present few, if any, clues of discontent, and only subtle ones at that. In all but the smallest organizations, however, a manager's contacts with employees are likely to be limited to an unrepresentative few and to be brief. Also, in an organization of any size, employee concern about the consequences of complaints is likely to deter all but the boldest or the most distressed.

Therefore the experience of no complaints could mean either that there is no major discontent or that employees are keeping their complaints to themselves. Should the latter be the case, there are only two ways to find out: by probing or by an explosion. Managements that do not hesitate to spend large sums on probing for remotely possible but potentially catastrophic physical defects (such as leaking valves) are often oddly reluctant to spend much smaller sums on probing for grievances whose cumulative effects are often serious and sometimes catastrophic. Disbelief that a problem exists in the absence of obvious, tangible evidence is only one cause of this reluctance. Other causes are detailed below.

—Employee complaints, when they are voiced at all, necessarily reflect only the employees' limited knowledge of matters about which management may have greater information than they do. (A common example is future plans for the utilization of facilities or equipment.) Hence management tends to dismiss the employee views as being ill-informed or likely to evaporate as soon as concrete evidence of management's real plan appears. Unfortunately, what exerts the behavioral effect on employees is not the question of whose views are right and whose are wrong, but the fact that one set of views is dismissed. The effect of not taking employee grievances seriously is simply to let the grievances become older, until prolonged unresponsiveness becomes in itself the most serious and damaging grievance.

—Astonishingly, some managements that are aware of a grievance will not avail themselves of the simple, and reasonably effective, device of explaining their view of the situation to the employees. The two most common rationalizations for this failure are that the facts will become obvious soon enough or that to acknowledge the existence of a grievance might create discontent among those employees who had not heard of it yet. Neither makes much sense (especially the latter, which is based on the naive notion that aggrieved persons are unaware of their problem until someone else tells them about it). As with all illogical actions by otherwise logical people, there is a deeper and not so readily rationalized reason underlying most such reluctance to discuss the grievance openly: that any employee grievance is a challenge to management's rectitude or wisdom and that the easiest (though least effective) way to cope with such challenges is to act as if they did not, or at least should not, exist.

—Finally, there is the other side of the power question: the side of the person who wields it. Power, whether it is formal or implicit, is an instrument. It is one of the tools of the trade, not a badge of office, a status symbol, or a license to abuse people. Most managers recognize this and look upon their power very much as a mechanic looks upon a wrench. But there are, regrettably, enough people in management for whom the job's power is its principal attraction, and these people make some kind of formal assurance against abuse almost mandatory.

By convincing itself that there either are or should be too few employee grievances to bother with, or that grievances must be based on inadequate information and will soon evaporate, or that overt challenges to management's competence or good intentions should not be encouraged by recognizing them, or that grievances threaten a precious prerogative that must be defended at all costs, managers too often guarantee that stage four will be reached —and, with a little bad luck thrown in—that stage five will be reached as well. The irony of it is that when explosive outbursts of employee dissatisfaction do occur, management, precisely because it has allowed itself to be oblivious to grievances, is very likely to be dumbfounded.

Grievance Channels: Unionized Companies

The detailed procedures specified in union contracts for processing grievances are usually second in importance only to the
economic and job security sections, as far as employees are concerned. They are also usually the only aspects of the contract to
have a day-to-day familiarity for most employees. Usually these
contracts provide a step-by-step procedure in which representatives of management and labor discuss grievances at progressively
higher levels, always trying (theoretically) to resolve them at the
lowest possible levels. If no resolution is possible between the
parties, the ultimate recourse is to arbitration—an expensive
procedure.

In practice, many grievances are settled not so much on their
merits as on the basis of "horse-trading"; each negotiator may be
willing to concede certain cases in order to win others. Thus
individual grievances tend to get caught up in the overall context
of company-union politics, and as a result individual grievants
may lose as easily as benefit. Sometimes internal union politics
may result in an unusually large number of grievances being
pushed to higher negotiating levels, as much to demonstrate
militancy to the membership as to harass management. For its
part, management (which typically is better able to afford
arbitration than the union) may balk at resolving certain issues
in the belief that the union will be unwilling to take the costly
risk of continuing its grievance to the ultimate stage. For these
reasons, the processing of grievances in unionized companies is
only roughly comparable to the civil justice system it theoretically
emulates.

The usual yardsticks for evaluating a unionized company's
grievance-handling procedure are the backlog of unresolved cases
and the percentage that are carried beyond the lowest levels of
discussion. If both figures are low, the system is considered relatively efficient, and the disposition of grievances is both swift and,
presumably, reasonably satisfactory in most cases. Heavy backlogs inevitably mean a lot of employees waiting a long time for
justice, or at least for a hearing. A large percentage of grievances
in the higher stages of discussion implies a lack of willingness to

deal with specific issues at lower levels— in itself probably a symptom of political discord within the union or between management and union.

Supervisors tend to be somewhat cynical about grievance procedures, since cases often appear to be settled other than on their merits. Some also fear that a record of incurring too many grievances will be held against them by their superiors. For these reasons, they may tend to enforce rules only sporadically, either when exasperated or with particularly flagrant violations. But sporadic enforcement invites a charge of arbitrariness or discrimination, so harried supervisors may find themselves caught in a trap of their own making. That is, they enforce rules sporadically because they expect to lose appeals, and they lose appeals because they enforce rules sporadically.

Grievance backlogs are as much the result of managerial bureaucracy as of union intransigence, as the following case shows.

A railroad which had experienced very poor labor-management relations embarked on a policy of deliberately seeking to improve them. This initiative coincided with the arrival, from outside the company, of a new president and a new vice president for personnel. A number of steps were taken, and the eventual results were no doubt the collective results of all of them. For our purposes, however, two steps were of particular interest.

Because of the wide geographic dispersion of its operations, grievance processing at the local level was usually confined to only the first two steps (discussions between the shop steward and the supervisor, then between the union's local business agent and the supervisor's boss). The company had found it too costly to maintain a trained labor relations staff at each of its regional offices. Consequently, any grievance that was not settled locally went directly to corporate headquarters, where it joined an enormous logjam of other grievances awaiting discussion with representatives of the various unions' international offices. The volume of incoming grievances exceeded the processing capability of the system—not because the grievance rate per se was high but because so large a number of sources funneled directly to a single processing point. As a result, delays of up to two years were by no means uncommon, and employees were convinced that management was deliberately dragging its feet in order to frustrate them.

The incoming vice president ordered the development of small, highly trained "flying squads" of company negotiators who traveled from location to location with full powers to settle grievances on his behalf. They were, in effect, mobile extensions of his negotiating authority. While these negotiating teams obviously increased the vice president's budget, the cost was not nearly as great as permanent stationing of negotiators in regional offices would have been. More importantly, the backlog of grievances was whittled down, grievance processing was speeded up, and employees began to recognize that the new management was making a genuine effort to be fair. Further, the vast majority of grievances dealt with by the mobile teams were comparatively minor matters which neither required nor benefited from high-level intervention.

As the vice president studied the patterns in the settlements worked out by his mobile teams, it became clear that a disproportionate number of grievances were related to the use of arbitrary, heavy-handed tactics by a limited number of supervisors. The old system had actually protected such supervisors, since it took a long time for their decisions to be reviewed and since few of them were ever reversed. The vice president reached a tough decision; the most flagrant of these heavy-handed supervisors simply had to go.

His reasoning was as follows. It was probably unrealistic to hope to reconstruct their approach to supervision, and any such attempt would take far too long to achieve the effects that were needed. Two effects were vital, and the only practical way to achieve either, he felt, was to relieve these individuals of their supervisory authority. One goal he sought was a dramatic example to all other supervisors that the days when management would protect harsh, authoritarian supervisors were over. The other goal was a vivid demonstration to employees that the railroad was now genuinely committed to fair, harmonious relations with them.

As a result of these and other actions, the levels of distrust and suspicion between management and its employees (and, indirectly, between management and the unions) began to wane. The most concrete evidence of this improved relationship came after a few years, when the railroad succeeded in negotiating a reduction in certain restrictive work practices which nearly every other railroad in the country continues to endure.

Grievance Channels: Nonunion Companies

Less than one out of four American workers are unionized, but the psychological forces that create the need for grievance channels affect virtually all workers. A variety of methods have evolved to provide for this need; some are passive, and others are active. Generally speaking, the active methods offer better protection against the development of a "stage four" condition, but they are also costlier and require greater sophistication than the passive methods.

The most common passive methods for dealing with grievances are responses to random complaints and the "open door" policy. The most common active methods are the use of "ombudsmen" and attitude surveys.

A "random" complaint is often peculiar to the grievant and does not affect any larger group of employees. It comes to management's attention for largely fortuitous reasons. For example, an executive may encounter an employee in a hallway, attempt to exchange pleasantries, and receive an earful in reply. Or someone with a claim on the executive's friendship (for example, a former colleague) may bring his own or someone else's complaint to the executive's attention. In some cases, a letter will arrive on the executive's desk (frequently unsigned) full of accusations about a particular department or manager. Unsigned letters are particularly difficult to cope with, since they are inherently unfair and often imply a certain imbalance on the part of the writer; but they may also be true.

The intuitive reaction of most managers when they encounter a random complaint is often to intervene, especially if the grievant has wisely chosen an executive who fancies himself as a paternalistic champion of "the little guy." However, the costs of such heroics often outweigh the benefits. Supervisors are likely to feel that their authority has been undermined and that further circumventions have been encouraged. Since the problems revealed by the complaint are likely to be isolated, any managerial action is likely to be perceived as overreaction.

Probably the wisest course is to refer the employee to his or her own immediate management and—if the case seems important enough—to direct that it be quietly investigated. Intervention is appropriate only if there is clear evidence that the complaint is not isolated but part of a larger pattern.

Some companies have established "open door" policies, which encourage any aggrieved employees who cannot receive satisfaction from their immediate superior to appeal their case to the next highest level of management, and if necessary even further. Such plans explicitly protect the employees from jeopardy, and in some cases their immediate superior is not aware that a grievance has been filed—unless, of course, it results in a reversal of a decision. Usually, some high-ranking executive, such as the vice president for personnel or even the president, serves as a final arbiter. Labor unions view such systems as inherently unfair, since management sits in judgment on its own members and there is no guarantee of a genuine adversary relationship.

Nevertheless, the system seems to "work" for many of the companies that use it, in the sense that relatively few grievances become generalized to large groups of employees. This is perhaps more likely to be true when management explicitly puts the burden of proof on the supervisor rather than on the aggrieved employee. However, this kind of discipline obviously presupposes a mature and highly professional supervisory group.

The "ombudsman" borrows a Scandinavian concept (and word) for seeking out and trying to rectify grievances, instead of waiting for them to manifest themselves either randomly or in a "stage five" outburst. Ombudsmen are representatives of higher management with the power to investigate, and often to rectify, employee complaints. Not only are they accessible to anyone who wants to lay a case before them, but they also visit the various departments and locations of the company to seek out problems. Sometimes the ombudsman interviews random samples of employees, and anyone who wishes to be included in this interview schedule is accommodated.

Although much of the ombudsmen's work consists of clarifying policies and offering advice, they are well positioned to detect grievances that (like most) have been concealed, and more importantly to detect patterns of grievances. As a rule it is only the latter that they report to higher management, usually with a recommendation for a policy change.

Because ombudsmen work on a face-to-face basis, they can

cover only a limited number of employees. On the other hand, the attitude survey can cover virtually all employees very quickly, excepting only those who are not present when the survey is taken or who are unwilling to participate. Surveys will be treated in greater detail in the chapter on morale; for the moment it suffices to point out that in addition to their speed and comprehensiveness, surveys offer the advantages of objectivity, diagnostic clues as to the reasons why attitudes develop, and comparability between successive surveys—which permits measurement of whether specific attitudes have improved or deteriorated in specific groups. The disadvantages of surveys are their cost, the temporary disruption of normal operations that they cause, and, perhaps most important, the expectations they arouse for some kind of tangible managerial responses to what they reveal.

All grievance-handling systems—with or without unions, passive or active—involve a circumvention of the immediate supervisor. A grievance is essentially an appeal for the reversal or modification of some supervisory action. Apart from whatever issues may be involved, a grievance almost always represents, at least potentially, a confrontation between two wounded egos— that of the grievant and that of the supervisor whose wisdom and/ or fairness is being challenged. The potential for damage to either or both egos, and to the constituency from which each individual is drawn, is always menacingly present. Hence all grievances are delicate matters that can be made worse by indelicate handling. Small wonder that many organizations prefer not to risk stirring up trouble with active systems of grievance processing, and that some prefer to have no system at all.

But reticence, in this instance, is not wisdom. Grievances are nettles that are easier to grasp—and to accept the pain—than to ignore. The issue of undermining supervisors needs to be faced squarely. No organization can afford to give even the most trusted supervisor the right to act independently of review and, when necessary, reversal. The mere opportunity for abuse can be every bit as damaging as abuse itself. Power is tolerable to those over whom it is wielded only when it is both limited and checked.

Supervisors who find these realities too unpalatable are saying, in effect, that they are unwilling to pay the price for the right to exercise power; and no organization can tolerate that. Like it or not—and it is probably "not" in most cases—the checks on supervisory power that are inherent in grievance processing are an indispensable component of effective management.

Chapter 9
Performance Appraisal

Few, if any, aspects of management reveal as disappointing a gap between potential and actuality as does performance appraisal. Under certain conditions, performance appraisal can contribute to such laudable goals as personal development, motivation and performance improvement, better morale, identification of promotable employees, determination of training needs, and even a fair and decent way to determine whether someone whose performance is weak should continue to hold a job. That is no mean list.

The problem is that those "certain conditions" are seldom created. To make matters worse, many organizations act as if they were unaware of them. All too frequently, the result is an impasse between managers (who claim that the appraisal instruments they are given to work with are unworkable) and personnel departments (who feel that their line managers are too naive to use the forms properly). There are elements of truth in both views, but on balance it would appear that personnel departments commit the greater error. It is the system itself, not the forms or the managers who are supposed to use them, that is chiefly at fault.

Nearly every organization has a performance appraisal "program." Typically, it consists of some impressively printed forms bound between expensive vinyl covers and distributed to all managers, along with some training on how to use them—and very little else. If the forms used by one company are compared with those of another, there is often a striking resemblance; and that is no accident. They are often copied from each other, since the criterion of being already in use typically carries far more weight than appropriateness or evidence of usefulness. The degree of intellectual mimicry between personnel departments with respect to performance appraisal is scandalous. In most cases the principal creative touches to distinguish one company's forms from another's are efforts to find less trite adjectives to express the same unworkable ideas.

Not surprisingly, most of these programs are highly susceptible to chronic disuse. From time to time, therefore, they may require the support of executive decrees that they *will* be used; and for a while after each such decree, they are. At most other times, they are not. Thus the paradox of performance appraisal is that nearly everyone favors their purposes and quarrels with their methods, to an extent that they are often reduced, in practice, to discarded formalities.

The problem of reconciling the need for performance appraisal with its sporadic practice is not insoluble, and the proof is that some organizations have solved it. They have done this by making their programs more realistic and workable, though certainly not more mandatory, than others. But solutions first require understanding, and the problem becomes more understandable when we consider the differing needs, and the assumptions of how best to satisfy those needs, of line managers and personnel departments.

For their part, line managers look to performance appraisal primarily for a means of dealing with inadequate performers. Some hope to help individuals raise their output above the marginal level. Probably a greater number merely want an appeal-proof case for firing or for transferring an individual out of their department. On the other hand, line managers are *not* interested in procedures which have the potential for undermining their current and foreseeable relationships with their subordinates.

Personnel departments have longer-range and more abstract goals for performance appraisal. They are concerned with minimizing the number of employees who ultimately find themselves trapped in positions that lead nowhere, or who live with the illusion that their work has been satisfactory when in fact it has not, or who appeal against demotion, transfer, or firing on the grounds that for years the work that is now found wanting has been accepted. (The common catch-phrase that expresses these goals is that employees must "know where they stand.") In a more positive vein, personnel departments are concerned with whether employees know what they can do to improve their pay or promotion prospects, whether talent is being identified and developed, and whether pay is related to performance.

The perspectives of the designers and users of performance appraisal are therefore quite different. It is hardly surprising if what is supplied does not satisfy the demand. But the problem is far worse than that, because what is supplied would not, in most cases, achieve its design objectives even if it were used, while what is demanded cannot be supplied. Thus the perspectives of the designers and users of conventional performance appraisal systems are not only inconsistent with each other, but both are out of touch (to varying degrees) with reality. Before we can hope to achieve the undeniably laudable goals of performance appraisal, we must think through the fundamentals of what we hope to accomplish, of why existing systems have counterproductive effects, and of how these can be avoided or at least mitigated.

The Goals of Performance Appraisal

Broadly speaking, there are two classes of goals toward which performance appraisal is aimed: administrative and behavioral.

Administrative goals are related to actions which management may wish to take relative to employees. Behavioral goals are related to actions which management may wish employees to take relative to themselves. These goals are usually poorly matched and often incompatible; to the extent that one is achieved, the other may be precluded. Yet most performance appraisal systems set out to accomplish both kinds of goals simultaneously, and as a result it is rare for either to be accomplished well.

The *administrative goals* of performance appraisal are concerned with the extremes of performance and with pay. In nearly all organizations during any given time period, the great majority of employees are doing their jobs "well enough"—neither extremely well nor extremely badly. Conservatively, at least 85 percent are ordinarily performing somewhere in the broad, "nonextreme" range. Thus the administrative goals are concerned at any given time with a small minority of employees (except, of course, for pay, which concerns all of them whenever pay is reviewed).

At the upper end of the performance spectrum, performance appraisal aims to identify persons who are promotable, qualified for special assignments, or deserving of special rewards (such as bonuses). At the lower end, it aims to identify those who need special help, as well as those who may have to be removed from their assignments or even from the payroll.

With regard to pay, few companies expect an exact correlation between performance and the size of an increase. The appraisal and the pay decision are not always made at the same time, and factors other than performance can affect pay decisions. Attitude, effort, and even age can enter the pay decision. (For example, when pension formulas are related to pay in the years immediately preceding retirement, increases in those years solely to increase pensions are by no means unusual.) Despite these exceptions, personnel departments tend to use performance appraisals as a rough check on whether the merit pay system is doing what it is supposed to do: reward high performance more than average performance, and average more than low.

To best achieve these administrative goals, the performance appraisal system must solicit inherently subjective judgments, which must be readily processable by clerks or computers. As a rule it is only practical to seek such judgments in confidence, since they are awkward to defend and can disrupt relationships if they are revealed. Hence the individuals who are the subjects of these judgments are seldom aware of them, much less permitted to question or rebut them, until and unless some action is taken. Even then they are unlikely to know the reasons for the action in any detail. For administrative purposes, then, the subjects of appraisal are excluded from the process and are only aware, if at all, of its ultimate results.

As for processing, this is easiest with a simple, standard nomenclature. Subtleties, extenuating circumstances, differentiating characteristics—the sorts of things that employees and at least the more sensitive supervisors are likely to consider quite important—are superfluous. Hence the lamentable trend to sorting everyone into a limited number of vaguely-defined categories, as if the world were really that simple. In sum, for purely administrative purposes a secret, arbitrary, bureaucratic system is easiest. But no surer prescription for failure to reach the behavioral goals of performance appraisal could possibly be written.

The behavioral goals are, first of all, to cope with the issue of everyone "knowing where they stand." More specifically, they are intended to allay fears of undisclosed disadvantages or jeopardy where there are none, and to assure awareness of them where there are, in order to either facilitate the correction of deficiencies or to justify whatever administrative action may be taken. The underlying idea is that all employees whose performance is found wanting have a right to know this, both so they can try to improve and so they can appeal if they consider the judgment unfair.

It is important to recognize that any instance of perceived performance deficiency by management represents, at least potentially, a grievance on the part of the employee. It is regrettably true that precisely to avoid awkward confrontations over such grievances, managers have often been less than candid about them. The result is that any eventual action—such as a deferred or limited pay increase—comes as a shock and thus becomes an even bigger grievance. The effects often spread beyond the individual grievant, creating fears of undisclosed criticisms and future injustice on the part of many other employees. To prevent such damage to morale, performance appraisal systems seek to compel candor as soon as it is called for and before it becomes inescapable.

The remaining behavioral goals are related to development. They include the identification of promotable talent, exceptional performance deserving of reward, and training needs. They also include the monitoring of individual development and a basis for coaching and counseling. These functions are best carried out if they are based on specific events, many of which cannot be anticipated and do not necessarily fall into predetermined categories. To rely on general descriptions or laudatory adjectives, while not uncommon, is comparatively useless. Thus the developmental goals of performance appraisal are best achieved by tailoring an approach to the circumstances and developmental pace of each individual.

We can now recapitulate the features that favor the administrative and behavioral purposes of performance appraisal. For administrative purposes, secret, arbitrary, and bureaucratic procedures are easiest. For behavioral purposes, candid, flexible, and tailored methods work best. Both purposes are necessary, but in view of their underlying incompatibility it is unwise, to say the least, to attempt to accomplish both simultaneously in a single program. The obvious solution is to separate them.

Separate Programs

At any given moment, the overwhelming majority of employees are in no particular need of administrative attention. They are not about to be promoted, recognized, rewarded, transferred, demoted, warned, or fired. Except for scheduled pay reviews, they are not about to receive a pay increase either. Thus, for most people most of the time, the administrative goals *and methods* of performance appraisal can simply be dispensed with, because the only realistic purposes are behavioral.

The performance level of the great majority of employees at any given time is somewhere in that broad range that can best be described as "good enough." The answer to the question of "where they stand" is that their performance is good enough to place them out of jeopardy. By far the best way of conveying this fundamental fact is to simply say so. Nothing more bureaucratic than a card with something like the following caption is needed:

Your job performance during the period just ended has been satisfactory. Let's meet in my office next Tuesday afternoon to discuss your views about your work, your career, and what we both can do during the next period to help achieve both your goals and the company's goals.

The traditionalist will find at least three aspects of this simplified approach amiss. First, there is no provision for different degrees of satisfactory performance; the barely passable is lumped together with the almost superb. Second, the individual's weaknesses and faults are not pointed out. Third, the responsibility for planning the discussion, and its outcome, is turned over to the subordinate.

By long tradition, most performance appraisal systems provide five rating categories. The middle one is supposed to represent an average of "most commonly expected" level of performance, and the others represent varying degrees of divergence above or below this presumably expected level. The underlying assumption is of a normal ("bell-shaped") probability distribution. In practice, the two extreme ratings (far above and far below average) are used so rarely as to be oddities, and the five theoretical categories become, for all practical purposes, three. The reasons are simply that extreme ratings may need to be defended and/or acted upon, neither of which the line manager is inclined to do, since either can disrupt the department. Further, the distribution within these middle three categories is seldom symmetrical but rather is skewed toward the high performance side. If performance ratings are to be believed, there are more people above average than at or below it—mathematically absurd but managerially quite possible.

As a rule, performance ratings are more reliable (in the sense that different raters will agree) the farther the ratings are removed from average. This means that the borderline areas (between average and above average, or between average and below average) tend to be clogged with arbitrary, unreliably classified cases. The existence of these two indistinctly differentiated border zones on either side of the range of common expectation is not so much the result of how performance actually distributes itself as it is of managerial motivation. It provides a marvelous opportunity to express personal preferences with impunity; it also warns the weak performers and titillates the strong ones without any commitment to either. The above and below average categories increase the manager's flexibility to avoid hard decisions, including the stigma implied in branding anyone as what most people obviously are: average.

Thus the harder one looks at the two rating categories adjacent to the center, the less justified they seem to be. This becomes especially clear if we ask what developmental purpose they serve, since that is the principal criterion for judging any aspect of performance appraisal when performance itself is not extreme. To suggest that people who are told they are below average will be motivated to improve does not square well with the facts; they are more likely to quarrel (at least in their own minds) with the rating. Being told one is above average is less likely to reinforce good habits or motivate a drive toward excellence than to make one suspect the rater of being constitutionally incapable of recognizing excellence when he or she sees it. In brief, if performance is not extreme and the main goal is therefore development, one broad "satisfactory" label on everyone's performance avoids a thicket full of contention. The object of the exercise is not the label but the growth of which the individual may still be capable.

The idea that performance appraisals should point out the individual's weaknesses rests on five assumptions, none of which survive close examination. The first assumption is that everyone has weaknesses. The point is too abstract to be debated. But the only weaknesses that matter for developmental purposes are those that are remediable. Many are not. Common experience shows us that many performance deficiencies are lifelong and represent ingrained habits or personal limits.

Nothing is to be gained by urging people to become what they are not. Thus, asking a characteristically careless person to become meticulous is no more sensible than asking a short person to grow taller; in both cases we would be trying to overcome the momentum of a lifetime of learning and growth. The obvious exception is a relatively young adult who probably will change, with or without managerial urging. But the pace of such natural growth is glacial, and its direction is uncertain.

Another practical weakness in the argument that "everyone has a weakness" is the question of defining the weakness. It can be simply a virtue carried to an extreme (for example, a systematic and orderly work pattern that can on occasion result in officious, unresponsive job behavior). Quite often, the "weakness" is in the eye of the beholder—in effect, a manager may be objecting that someone else isn't sufficiently like himself.

Unless a "weakness" is perceived by a consensus of observers to be easily correctable by relatively minor conscious effort, little is to be gained by pointing it out. The manager may vent displeasure, the subordinate may be mortified, and the weakness will probably persist. The wiser course is to say nothing and either tolerate the weakness or, if it seriously impairs job performance, redesign the job or transfer the employee. (Remember, we are considering persons whose overall performance is satisfactory and for whom our primary goal is development. If the weakness were sufficient to render overall performance unsatisfactory, our primary goal would be administrative, and a different procedure would be appropriate.)

The second assumption is that all people want to overcome their weaknesses. But they may not regard the same thing as a weakness, or at least not as a serious one. If they do, they are probably already exerting what effort they can to overcome it. Further, since we usually point out other people's weaknesses in vague, abstract terms (mostly to minimize our own discomfort), they may be at a loss to know precisely what to do to please us. Not infrequently, they will conclude that we have some kind of mental set that compels us to stereotype them for rating purposes, regardless of what they may do. Sometimes—lamentably—they are right.

The truth of the matter, probably, is that most people are far more interested in reassurance that their jobs are secure and their prospects are favorable than in pleasing their boss by overcoming what he or she thinks of as a weakness. It is only when security or prospects are not assured that interest in doing something about weaknesses is likely to be aroused.

A third assumption is that individuals cannot improve their performance unless their weaknesses are pointed out to them. This assumes that the performance deficiency is due to their habits. However, it could also be due to faulty communication, low morale, inadequate training, lack of cooperation by other employees or departments, poor working conditions, a mismatch between talents or interests and job requirements, or several other possibilities. It also assumes that individuals *can* improve. As noted above, it would not be unusual if in fact they could not.

A fourth assumption is that a manager's diagnoses of a subordinate's weaknesses are valid and reliable. Some are and some are not. The quality of an individual's performance can be affected by the quality of the relationship with his or her superiors. We commonly experience relationships that bring out the best, or the worst, in us or others. Further, we know that tastes and rating standards vary from one manager to another. About the only thing we know for sure when a manager perceives a weakness in a subordinate is that he or she perceives it. Whether other observers would agree, or whether the manager is partially the cause of the weakness, is an open question.

A fifth assumption is that as a tactic for dealing with subordinates it is wise to be able to point out weaknesses. This allegedly keeps the subordinate focused on working hard to please the boss and deflects, or at least defers, any demands for recognition of superior performance. It is probably true that pointing out weaknesses puts the other person on the defensive and at least temporarily relieves the manager from having to cope with the subordinate's most important wishes. But the tactic is self-defeating, for in the long run it only nurtures grievances and motivates a search for subtle means of retaliation.

So much for the value of pointing out weaknesses. Turning over responsibility to subordinates for planning their own near-term development is more controversial. Obviously, there is considerable variation in both the ability and willingness of employees to take advantage of such an opportunity. However, the advantages of this approach outweigh its disadvantages.

Broadly speaking, most people fall into one of four groups with regard to the likelihood of their further development at any given time:

—those who are self-motivating and will probably continue to develop regardless of what is or is not done for them;

—those who with a minimum of encouragement and with fertile circumstances will probably take over responsibility for their own development;

—those who will develop, if at all, only with continual support and guidance; and

—those who, for whatever reason, will develop no further.

The second and third groups are of greater practical importance than the first and fourth. Obviously, the approach advocated here is aimed chiefly at the second, usually quite large, group, whose members are likely to develop farther and faster under their own guidance than under anyone else's. As for the third group, the main problem is to positively identify them, and if this approach is used they tend to sort themselves out readily enough. They are the ones who persistently fail to produce a coherent plan for themselves or to follow through with their plans.

Thus a separate, nonevaluative performance evaluation program is feasible for the vast majority of employees who really don't need evaluation. That leaves us free to establish a separate, administratively-oriented program for the minority who do need it, and thus to deal with individuals in the way that most of them prefer—individually. The need for acquiring skills in communication, diplomacy, and even psychotherapy (that most managers are incapable of acquiring) vanishes. The solution to the performance appraisal problem is not to do it better but to do it differently.

Involuntary Adversaries

If ratings must be given, it is better to give them on a *categorical* basis of having either met or not met a criterion than in terms of the *degree* to which a standard was met, missed, or exceeded. The distinction is essentially the same as between letter or numerical grades for students and a simple "pass-fail" system. The rating system itself turns out, somewhat surprisingly, to be at the root of much antagonism between supervisors and subordinates and between supervisors and the personnel departments that insist on the use of ratings.

The basic problem is with the vagueness with which the various rating categories are defined. Most rating systems attempt to express deviations around an average or expected level of performance but leave it entirely to the raters to determine what *average* or *expected* actually means. Or they may be asked to determine whether someone's performance has "met requirements" without being told exactly what those requirements are. Thus raters are thrust into the position of not only having to contrive their own rating criteria every time they evaluate someone's performance but also of having no defense against charges of inconsistency, capriciousness, or favoritism. Small wonder that supervisors feel performance appraisals for any but the extreme performers are potentially disruptive of working relationships, and try to either gloss over the process or avoid it altogether.

When supervisors are persuaded (or coerced) to use the system, they tend to develop a strategy aimed at preventing or minimizing harm to their relationship with subordinates. This often takes the form of brief, cursory discussions in which shortcomings are hinted at indirectly, if at all. The supervisors' objective is not to go into detail but to get a potentially awkward discussion over with as quickly as possible. When this approach is used, it is hardly surprising if employees develop the impression that their work is more highly rated than it is.

However, this approach may not work, since subordinates may ask for more information or for an explanation of why they were not rated higher. Realizing this possibility, supervisors are likely to develop a contingency plan. Their ratings are inherently open to challenge because they are based on an interpretation of what performance standards should be. So supervisors arm themselves with defenses of their ratings, which they usually use only if required to do so. These defenses tend to be selected instances of performance that did not meet expectations.

The supervisor's defense puts the subordinate at a serious disadvantage. The incidents cited may have occurred so many months before that the subordinate no longer recalls them in detail. He or she may have been given no reason, at the time, to regard them as especially significant and may argue that they are atypical; but that merely pits the subordinate's subjective judgment against that of the superior. Since the subordinate can seldom anticipate just how the boss will choose to buttress the ratings, he or she cannot prepare an adequate rebuttal in advance.

For all these reasons, subordinates are unlikely to press a challenge very vigorously, even if they vigorously disagree. The circumstances are tilted so decisively in the boss's favor that the risks in contention are seldom worth the gain. But while subordinates may protest only mildly, or not at all, they may *feel* aggrieved.

No supervisory skill or artistry is likely to preclude this. The problem is not with technique but with the system. It thrusts the supervisor and subordinate into an adversary relationship, forcing them into roles they probably would not select voluntarily. This is a major reason why performance evaluation has so often fallen so far short of its goals. Employees may be told where they stand, but it is far from certain that they understand, believe, or accept what they are told. To make matters worse, a quite workable relationship may be subtly undermined for weeks or even longer. And the irony of it is that this unfortunate outcome, which is by no means rare, derives from the very concept of rating performance in the absence of clear-cut, objective guidelines.

Attempts to solve the problem semantically, by phrasing the rating categories more precisely—or graphically, by altering the layout of the rating form—are futile. They do not cope with the central problem, which is the necessity of each supervisor establishing his or her own standards of what is "average," "expected," or "required" of each subordinate. To the extent that performance evaluation must be converted into paper work, the best form in most cases is a blank piece of paper. The supervisor and subordinate can record on it whatever standards of performance they agree on (or in the case of unsatisfactory performance, standards of improvement that the supervisor insists on). In all cases they would be wise to avoid further semantic traps by eschewing *descriptions* of performance (adjectives, adverbs, and ratings) altogether, and to refer instead to the specific outcomes or results which, if they occur, would constitute satisfactory evidence of satisfactory performance. The subordinate would then know exactly what to aim for and exactly how the performance will be measured, without having to analyze the boss's value systems or semantic habits. In most such cases the subordinates will know "where they stand," and what they can do about it, before the boss does.

What is advocated here as a substitute for performance ratings is a variant on the "management by objectives" system popularized in recent years by several management authorities (notably Drucker, Humble, and Odiorne). It is a powerful technique that can circumvent many of the unfortunate side-effects of conventional performance evaluation. But it has limitations of its own, and it is important to review the most significant of them.

The term *management by objectives* (often abbreviated to "MBO") is a bit unfortunate, since the word *objective* is both a noun (meaning a goal) and an adjective (meaning susceptible of the same evaluation independently of any particular evaluator). MBO is typically thought of as a system of assigning goals; but unless the goals themselves are expressed objectively, the same semantic traps that plague rating systems are encountered again.

The criterion of an effective goal-setting under MBO is that any informed observer would give the same categorical yes-or-no answer to the question of whether it had, or had not, been attained.

In practice, it is frequently difficult—but not impossible—to reduce the most important aspects of a job to a few results which can be expressed unequivocally and which are not, at the same time, trivial. What is really called for is thinking the job through to its consequences and distinguishing what is essential from what is merely important or helpful.

However, effective goal-setting is not a mere question of proper phrasing. It is also vital that the objectives be perceived as attainable by the person who is supposed to attain them. The awkward fact of human nature that has to be contended with here is that most people feel little or no commitment to goals which in their view are imposed on them. An imposed goal is likely to be perceived by the person who is supposed to achieve it as arbitrary, unrealistic, and unfair. The chances are therefore very good that the person won't try very hard to achieve it and will regard the failure as no failure at all but rather as a vindication of his or her views. On the other hand, if the goal is perceived as reasonable, attainable, and fair, it is more likely to elicit effort and, consequently, to be achieved. The circumstances in which people are most likely to consider a goal to be reasonable, attainable, and fair are when they have helped to set it, or at least have influenced it.

It follows that in addition to being expressed in unequivocal terms, goals have to be negotiated. This injects an unfamiliar degree of equality into a traditionally unequal relationship, but the purpose has nothing whatever to do with lofty theories of industrial democracy. Rather it is a matter of accommodating a managerial system to fit human nature. This is sometimes difficult to do, but it is surely preferable to the opposite, which is impossible.

Accommodating the System to People

The goals of performance evaluation can be (and have been)

met when the conditions are right. We can now summarize these
conditions.

—Separate programs are needed for those who need administrative attention and those who need only reassurance and
development. Most contemporary performance evaluation
programs are appropriately designed for administrative purposes and can be used with little modification where they are
appropriate. However, for most people most of the time, a
nonbureaucratic, customized approach based on reassurance,
counseling, and goal-setting is more appropriate.

—The most effective solution to the problem of supervisory skill
in communicating details of evaluation to subordinates is to do
away with the need for skill by doing away with the details.
One broad category of "satisfactory performance," without
degrees of "satisfactoriness" or explanations of why performance is satisfactory, can accommodate the great majority of
employees.

—Performance evaluation can usefully be converted to performance planning and individual goal-setting. At the very least
this approach avoids the problem of "involuntary adversaries"
and its unfortunate chain of consequences. At best, it can help
to motivate superior performance and continued personal
growth.

Chapter 10
Morale

The morale of individuals or groups is a kind of summary statement of all the various psychological forces impinging on them with respect to their work. If on balance the effect is positive, job performance will tend to be enhanced. For example, adverse circumstances, such as severe weather, may be dealt with superbly. On the other hand, if the balance of forces is negative, the effect may be a detraction from job performance. For example, quality may be ignored, customers slighted, and costs allowed to escalate.

However, these effects are usually subtle and become significant chiefly when morale approaches an extreme. Most of the time, morale is neither very positive nor very negative, which is why management usually ignores it or takes it for granted. But even when its effects are unobtrusive, morale may be *moving toward* one extreme or the other, usually with a glacial speed that accelerates only as the extreme is approached. This is why management's concern with morale is usually confined to those periods when it has become so negative that it motivates very costly behavior, such as a strike or excessive turnover.

As a result, much of what we know about morale is derived from psychological "postmortems" (commonly known as morale surveys or attitude surveys), in which behavioral scientists have tried to reconstruct a catastrophe after the fact. This chapter is based largely on the results of such surveys, primarily because of their instructional value—which should not be misconstrued as advocating their wider use. Under the right circumstances, morale surveys can be very valuable. But those circumstances are not common, and as we shall see, this dictates that they be used only selectively. Some less sophisticated but far more widely applicable methods of assessing morale will be described toward the end of the chapter.

The following case illustrates both the power and the hazards of the survey technique of diagnosing morale.

A large manufacturer of farm equipment endured a strike of nearly three months' duration at one of its major plants. The effects were nothing less than catastrophic for everyone concerned.

Employees lost nearly a quarter of their annual pay. Their chances of recovering any significant part of this loss were virtually nil, since the contract for which they eventually settled provided only minor wage gains. Many had depleted their savings, and some had to borrow heavily simply to meet everyday expenses. The huge loss in their aggregate purchasing power impacted the local merchants most severely, causing a number to go out of business.

The company lost not only three months of production but also domestic customers and several very sizable export orders to competitors, all as a direct consequence of the strike. Thus its sales base and market share after the strike ended were considerably smaller than before it began. Profits for the year were down sharply, also as a direct result of the strike.

When the crisis had finally passed, a number of key executives began to look beyond the issues on the bargaining table in order to understand why such a costly event had occurred. They reasoned that since the contract which the employees eventually accepted was only marginally better than the one they had rejected before the strike began, something more important than a few cents per hour must have been involved. As a result of their conjectures, two main hypotheses emerged, each of which had a number of advocates among the ranks of higher management.

The first theory, which was supported by most of the plant's managers, was that a combination of internal union politics and employee naiveté was to blame. They pointed to a power struggle between rival factions in the union. The faction that was then out of power had accused the union's officers of being duped by—and even of secretly collaborating with—management and of willingness to settle for much too disadvantageous a contract. Because of these attacks, the faction in power (so the theory went) felt it had to demonstrate its militancy by rejecting what the plant's managers considered a quite reasonable contract and by allowing the strike to grind on until no one could tolerate it any longer. Further, this theory proposed that most employees had probably been deceived by union oratory into thinking that the strike-ending contract was a victory, when actually it simply cut their losses without any possibility of restoring them.

The second theory was held chiefly by managers at corporate headquarters. (A subtle but important point in this case is that the plant in question had served as a sort of "training academy" for future corporate executives; and many managers at headquarters were "graduates," so to speak, of the stricken plant.) This view stressed the fact that the strike was the first in the plant's twelve-year history and that, until it erupted, the plant had always been considered a model of positive labor-management relations. Something must have happened to undermine the previously healthy climate, the headquarters managers reasoned. There had been virtually no change in the employee group or in the makeup of the union leadership, while plant management had undergone constant turnover due to transfers and promotions in and out. Therefore, the theory at corporate headquarters was that the fault must lie with the current crop of plant managers. Looking back on their own pleasant relationships with employees and union alike, the headquarters executives concluded that the current plant management had lost the "common touch" and must have been dealing with employees in an impersonal, bureaucratic way.

Not surprisingly, the managers at the plant disputed the headquarters view as being unrealistic, based on conjecture, and self-serving to boot. The existence of factional strife within the union was an established fact, while any loss of managerial "common touch" was pure conjecture.

However, much more was at stake in this debate than mere theories or internal managerial politics. The strike had been terribly costly, and to prevent its repetition management needed to base its plans on the explanation that best fitted the facts. For this reason, an independent study was commissioned about six weeks after the strike ended. This study was based on confidential interviews with a 10 percent cross-sectional sample of the plant's employees, followed by a questionnaire (based partially on the interview findings) which was completed by everyone present and willing to do so during a two-day period—about 90 percent of the total plant population.

Piecing together the various parts of the puzzle, the study group tried to differentiate the *precipitating* causes (or "triggers") of the strike—the dollars-and-cents issues of wage negotiations)—from the *predisposing* causes which made the employees susceptible not only to walking out but to staying out for nearly three months. They concluded that while both the plant and the headquarters theories were at least partially true, neither dealt with the heart of the problem. The basic difficulty, as they saw it, was that the plant was twelve years old!

A heavy majority of the employees had been hired within a year or two of the plant's opening and had been employed long enough to rise to the top of their wage brackets. The only way for them to continue improving their status—in terms of both income and job satisfaction— was to transfer into a more highly-rated job. Here the plant's administrative rigidities got in the way. Openings of this kind were seldom publicized, since managers preferred to choose their own new subordinates rather than have to consider applicants whom they might not know or like. To make matters worse, many of the employees who were unable to advance were trapped in particularly unattractive jobs (involving intense heat, smoke, and constant danger of being burned on the hands and arms), which had previously been tolerable chiefly because one could look forward to promotion.

Thus one of the predisposing causes of the strike was the accumulated frustration of large numbers of employees who were unable to escape from jobs which did not meet their needs for either money or for safe, enjoyable work. They would find out about job openings for which they might have wished to apply only after the jobs had been filled; and they came to the almost universal conclusion that favoritism, rather than qualifications, determined one's fate at the plant. On that particular point, the study team had to agree that the grievance was largely justified.

An interesting feature of the questionnaire data was the surprisingly high percentage of employees who felt that the plant was an extremely dangerous place to work—surprising because the accident rate actually compared rather favorably with that of similar plants in the area. Nevertheless, many employees came to work each day with the grim, resigned attitude of infantrymen slogging onto a battlefield. True, there had been a few severe accidents, but these seemed inadequate to explain so strong a reaction.

Getting to the bottom of this mystery required the use of a computer and an elaborate mathematical procedure which compared the answer to each question with the same individual's answers to all other questions. The aim was to discover which attitudes tended to cluster together with the feeling that the plant was excessively unsafe. Another surprise then emerged. The feelings of danger tended to coincide with resentment of pressure for production, of a tendency for each shift to compete with the other two, and with a feeling that management cared only about the quantity and not the quality of the materials that were produced.

Management had, in fact, deliberately encouraged a policy of competition between shifts and was firmly convinced that it helped stimulate production. What they did not reckon with was that the employees, under pressure from the supervisors to outproduce the other two shifts, would find it easier to handicap the other shifts rather than to excel them. Thus they hid expensive tools and parts, making them unvailable to the other shifts. Each shift did the easiest work available and left the more difficult tasks for the incoming shift. They kept vital information to themselves, leaving the next shift in the dark. Thus the production gains were bought at a high price. The illogic of it all was more apparent to the employees than to their supervisors, who chose not to notice these practices—or to higher management, which was evidently oblivious to them.

Hence the feeling that management was more interested in quantity than quality is understandable. Relating this to the apparently exaggerated fear of accidents required but another step: linking the apparently illogical pressure for production-at-any-price to management's apparent unconcern with the blocked ambitions of so many of its employees. Evidently many employees were convinced that management was obsessed with production and concerned with them only as instruments of production. In brief, management didn't seem to care about them.

The tendency of employees to exaggerate the number and severity of accidents was a simple extension of the underlying conviction that management was using them as mere pawns. There were, as one might suspect, some instances of unsafe practices, and these tended to be interpreted as examples both of managerial callousness and of the results of excessive pressure to produce. Instances of such conditions (for example, frayed cables), although rare, were widely discussed and cited as further proof that "the company doesn't care."

The predisposition to strike probably developed over a period of several years, during which the feeling became widespread that management was utterly uninterested in employees' most serious concerns. This belief was not the result of harsh or rude tactics by individual supervisors (which were evidently quite rare). It was due instead to the slow growth of a condition which had not existed in earlier years (blocked advancement) and to management's neglect of this condition and its seemingly irrational preoccupation with production.

The strike was apparently not motivated by the simple desire to call attention to a grievance, since the grievance had long since passed that stage. It was precipitated by a convenient economic issue and a convenient intra-union squabble; but the reason why these sparks were able to provoke a strike in the first place, and the reason why the strike lasted as long as it did, was that the employees needed to assuage their sense of gross injustice. The strike ended when they had vented their spleen. (We thus see in this case the classic evolution of a grievance through five stages, from inception to explosion, as outlined in Chapter 8.)

Interviews revealed that employees were aware that the strike had cost them heavily and gained them little in purely economic terms. They had not been duped by union oratory (or management oratory either). But in their view, economic factors were secondary. The primary consideration, as they saw it, was that management had been taught a painful lesson: that it couldn't "push its employees around" with impunity. The strike was a retaliation that was necessary to restore the offended employees' pride. Thus from their perspective, the strike was well worth what it had cost them.

Armed with this analysis by the study group, management undertook to develop a program of preventive action through rebuilding morale and employee confidence in the wisdom and fairness of management. Sad to relate, these efforts foundered. A proposal to post all job openings, so that qualified employees could bid for them, was successfully opposed on the grounds that it would add paperwork and make it awkward for management to select the "best qualified" individuals. The effect was to restrict candidacy for promotion to those individuals already known to and liked by their supervisors—a clear exposure to favoritism (or at least to continuing charges of favoritism).

A proposal to end the deliberate stimulation of shift competition was eventually talked to death; too many middle-managers had a vested interest in sustaining it, and too many supervisors were accustomed to it. A proposal to alter the inspection system so that defects would be called to the attention of the supervisor in whose department they were created was abandoned as uneconomical.

Thus none of the underlying causes of the strike were addressed at all. But management did act quite decisively with regard to a symptom; it purchased an expensive new ambulance, which was stationed near the plant gate as clear demonstration of its concern for prompt care in case of injury.

In fairness to the managers concerned, it must also be noted that many of them were unconvinced by psychological explanations such as these and preferred to believe that internal union politics were largely or even entirely to blame for the strike. Hence, from their perspective, none of the proposed actions were necessary. This kind of skepticism is not unusual; it is one of the constant hazards of the applied psychologist's trade.

One of the most important lessons to emerge from retrospective analyses of this kind is that they should not be undertaken unless management is committed in advance to taking action addressed to the underlying causes of low morale. Otherwise the expectations of already frustrated people are raised only to be dashed. The analysis can, in other words, harm its subjects if the findings are not used. Therefore, a prerequisite to morale analyses is a conviction on the part of management that the improvement of morale is of sufficient importance to be worth altering or abandoning some of the practices (usually undertaken for reasons quite unrelated to morale) that may have caused it to deteriorate.

Not all case histories of morale analyses end as disappointingly as this one did. The following two cases demonstrate the significant gains that are sometimes possible as a result of studies of this type.

A computer software company that provided a programming and systems analysis service to computer users began to experience a much higher than anticipated rate of turnover among its systems analysts. These were highly qualified specialists whose work was critically important to the total package of services that the company provided.

Since they were in the systems business themselves, the company's executives were accustomed to manpower planning and had, in fact, based their forecasts on the assumption of a moderately high turnover rate. Systems analysts were then in short supply and very much in demand, and it was only realistic, they felt, to anticipate some losses—this despite the company's best efforts to retain them. The problem was that a continuation of the higher actual rate of turnover would soon begin to hamper the company's efforts to serve its clients, much less to seek new ones.

The company's managers rejected the "obvious" explanation—that their systems analysts were leaving primarily because they could make more money elsewhere—because that did not explain why a majority of their systems analysts had not left. In the extremely competitive talent market that existed at that time, almost any systems analyst who was willing to swap a current job for higher pay elsewhere could do so. Management was convinced that the problem was more complex than a simple matter of pay but was at a loss to determine what else might be involved. Interviews with the systems analysts themselves produced almost as many theories as there were interviews.

A decision was made to undertake a morale survey. Due to the nature of their business, the company was familiar with the computer technique that makes it possible to determine which cluster of attitudes has a tendency to be associated with any other given attitude. Therefore they determined to seek out the underlying problems which, taken together, tended to produce a predisposition to seek employment elsewhere or to accept offers of employment. They were gambling, of course, that there really was some kind of underlying pattern and that the systems analysts were motivated by factors which they were either unaware of or could not articulate.

In this case, the gamble paid off (which doesn't always happen). The computer did find a group of questions which tended to be answered in the same ways by systems analysts who indicated an inclination to leave (by selecting the answer "I doubt I will still be working for this company one year from now"). But the cluster of attitudes associated with this answer was rather puzzling. For the most part, they involved the feeling that one's training was not being fully utilized or that one's professional (as distinct from financial) future seemed unsatisfactory. Attitudes toward pay actually showed no clear-cut relation to attitudes toward leaving or staying.

Computers do not solve problems of this kind. They can only indicate which clues are more likely than others to lead to a solution. But in a case like this, with an abundance of clues and no obvious pattern among them, the role of the computer was indispensable. It told the study group to examine the way in which systems analysts' training was utilized and how their careers were managed. As so often happens, this led to the discovery that the source of the problem lay in a management practice undertaken for reasons which (superficially, at least) had nothing whatever to do with morale and which had satisfactorily achieved the (nonmorale) goals the company had hoped to achieve.

Systems analysis requires an in-depth familiarity with the practices and problems of each industry in which it is applied. Acquiring this familiarity was rather time-consuming for any given analyst. Therefore, to maximize the time available for actual consulting with clients, management had decided to minimize the familiarization time of each analyst. This was done by having each analyst specialize in a given industry. As the turnover problem began to restrict the number of trained analysts available, management reacted by having them specialize still further. They did this by assigning analysts to a sequence of essentially similar computer applications within their industry.

From the standpoint of maximizing the availability of scarce manpower, the specialization technique made sense. In this case, however, it tended to conflict with one of the fundamental motivations for becoming a systems analyst in the first place: the desire to develop one's talents to the fullest. After several essentially similar assignments, the analysts began to find their work less satisfying. Without necessarily knowing why, they began to view their future pessimistically and to feel that their hitherto exciting, stimulating jobs were deteriorating toward the routine level of ordinary jobs. Turnover was not a *direct* result of this feeling, but it did provide the susceptibility to opportunities for change without which those opportunities would have aroused little interest.

It was clear that the "medicine," in this case, was making the "patient" worse. That is, by increasing specialization in response to the talent shortages induced by turnover, management was probably unintentionally stimulating turnover still further. At least that was the analysis presented by the study team; and in this case, management accepted it. To get the talent shortage under control, they took the conscious risk of temporarily worsening it by putting a limit on the number of essentially similar *consecutive* assignments any systems analyst could be given. Beyond that limit, the analyst had to agree before a further assignment of the same kind could be made; and beyond a further limit, the approval of a corporate vice president was necessary.

To interpose a bureaucratic procedure that limits managerial discretion is never welcome and seldom creative. But this was an exception. Managers saw the clear implication that specialization would seldom be feasible beyond the stated limits, and therefore they seldom attempted it. The initial result, as everyone had feared, was a decrease in job completions due to additional time spent in familiarization. However, the turnover rate also began a gradual decline, until eventually the entry rate of newly trained analysts (which had not increased) was sufficient to stabilize supply with demand. Thereafter, as turnover dropped still further (eventually approximating its original rate), the company was able to handle an expanded workload without resorting to excessive specialization.

A manufacturer of duplicating equipment provided a field maintenance and repair service to users of its products. As they expanded their sales (and, consequently, their maintenance service) into regions of the country where they had not operated previously, they encountered a unique problem. The maintenance men in the new regions were unable to attain the productivity levels of their counterparts in the older regions. This persisted for several years, so the problem could not be attributed to mere differences in experience levels. In the newer regions, the average number of repair and maintenance calls handled by the maintenance men remained stuck at about 20 percent below the average of the older regions. Management eventually came to accept this difference as a mysterious, frustrating, and essentially unchangeable fact of life.

There was no shortage of theories. One was that because of the "way of life" in the new region, the people there were "just naturally" slower than people in the older regions. It is true that there were differences in educational and economic levels in the regions as a whole. But the company's personnel department established that there were no differences in the average educational level of its maintenance men from one region to another; nor were there differences in their basic abilities—to the extent that these could be measured by aptitude tests. Some executives suspected that the maintenance men in the new region were deliberately slowing down their work, but repeated investigations turned up no supporting evidence. As the company's business in the new region expanded, the lower productivity rate constituted a serious drain on profitability.

Finally, one manager—newly assigned to this region—came across a clue. He noted that several of his men complained of extreme fatigue at the end of each day. As far as he could tell, the complaints were genuine. The men gave every appearance of being exhausted. Since they happened to live in a relatively small community, he could easily establish that they were in the habit of going directly home from work and retiring for the night at a relatively early hour.

Playing a hunch, the manager began checking with his colleagues in nearby districts. It soon developed that the pattern of fatigue was fairly widespread. Despite their lower productivity, the men were working very hard by their own standards—to the point of exhaustion. But the work was not physically taxing, and the manager saw no reason to suspect that the maintenance men in his region were less healthy than those in other regions.

At this point, all he had was an intriguing little mystery. He had no satisfactory explanations. But he was wise enough to realize that the clue could be valuable, so he brought it to the attention of his superiors. One of them decided to commission a morale study, in hopes of not only explaining the fatigue problem but of possibly linking it to the productivity problem as well.

The study team was basically looking for those attitudes or beliefs that predisposed certain maintenance men to complain of fatigue more than others did. Using the method already described, the team discovered that those maintenance men who complained the most of fatigue were also more likely than the rest to criticize the quality of their training and to note that the burden of their responsibilities weighed heavily on their minds, both on and off the job.

Following this line of evidence, the training program was reviewed. Although basic training was provided at the main manufacturing plant for maintenance men from all parts of the country, most further training —including advanced techniques, refresher courses, and introductions to new equipment—was carried out at regional centers. The instructors at these centers were maintenance men who were assigned to these duties for periods of two or three years before returning to field duties. They traveled to the main plant to be instructed themselves and then returned to their regions to train their colleagues. The system had worked well enough for years, and the question that the study team now raised with regional management was whether their training center might be different in some way from those of the other regions.

At first this seemed unlikely, but the study team persisted, simply because no other explanation seemed to fit the available evidence. Eventually it was noted that in selecting instructors for its centers, the management in this region had tended to assign its less

capable maintenance men, chiefly in order to keep the most
effective men in the field. Other regions, by contrast, had viewed
instructional assignments as a potential stepping-stone into
managerial or technically specialized jobs and had therefore tended to
prefer their more productive men for these positions. In both cases,
informal traditions rather than policies were involved.

The explanation offered by the study team for both the fatigue and
the lower productivity of this region was as follows. Although the
content of the training received by maintenance men in this region was
the same as that in other regions, the men did not develop the same
confidence in their training as did their colleagues in other regions. The
cause was a combination of comparatively unpersuasive instruction and,
perhaps more importantly, a lack of conviction by the maintenance men
that their instructors were properly informed themselves.

The result was an uncertainty that the lessons were properly
understood and a corresponding reluctance to make diagnostic judgments
in the field. To the extent that any individual maintenance man was
handicapped by this uncertainty, he would naturally tend to work more
slowly—double- and even triple-checking his ideas before committing
himself to a particular repair procedure—and also to worry more about
whether what he had done was in fact the best way to cope with the
problem he had faced.

Once again, a psychological explanation had emerged, based on the
unforeseen side-effects of a practice not directly related to morale—a
practice, moreover, that was satisfactorily achieving its intended purpose
(keeping the most skilled maintenance men in the field). The same
understandable skepticism and resistance to this explanation arose
among the managers of this region as had occurred among the managers
in the other cases cited. But the regional manager himself made the
decision to accept it as his best—indeed, his only—hope of ever bringing
the maintenance productivity of his region up to normal standards. He
directed that henceforth all new instructors for the regional training center
would be selected from among the most effective and promising
maintenance men in the region.

It took some time before the new policy could be fully implemented
and still more time before its effects could be felt. After all, those
of the maintenance men who had been pulling the region's
productivity average down were convinced, from long experience,
that the job itself was extremely difficult. Few, if any, of them
connected their low opinion of their training with their perception of
how difficult their jobs were. But as time went on, a gradual increase
in the region's productivity began to be observed. Whether it was a

direct effect of the change in the quality of instructors was, of
of course, debatable. The fact that one event precedes another does
not make the first a cause or the second an effect. But it is also true that
the productivity problem had remained intractable for several years
prior to the regional manager's action and that no other obvious
change had occurred to account for the improvement.

The factor that led to success in the two cases just cited was not
the study teams or their technique of analyzing questionnaire
responses with the aid of computers. Any competent graduate
student in the behavioral sciences, teamed with any competent
computer programmer, could have done what they did. In both
cases, the essential ingredient of success was a management that
was willing to trade away certain advantages (optimum manpower deployment) in order to cope with the underlying causes
of a morale problem—and perhaps even more important, willing
to gamble that a psychological explanation of that morale problem might be right.

Large-scale, serious morale problems are almost never the
result of heavy-handed, grossly abusive supervisory methods.
Such incidents still occur, of course, but for the most part they
are isolated relics of an era that has long since passed. Nevertheless, when costly morale problems do crop up, management has a
tendency to assume that either its own supervisors or a handful of
agitators are at fault. In most cases, however, regardless of
whether clumsy supervisors or clever agitators are at work, the
problems would not tend to reach significant levels if fundamental
human needs were being met. In the cases cited, these needs were
related to career progress (and its correlate, financial progress),
to job satisfaction, and to job competence. These are not the only
needs that, when blocked, can lead to severe morale difficulties;
but they do illustrate the depth and nature of the needs that are
likely to be involved.

In some companies, management tacitly acknowledges that
morale is poor and even that this may, to some extent, be the
indirect result of steps it has taken for the sake of efficiency. But
the morale problem is regarded as a tolerable, if regrettable, cost
of the efficiency gain. In other words, management chooses to
"live with" low morale and to try to offset its more costly conse-

quences with other (usually technological) sources of productivity. No general statement is possible as to whether this is wise or unwise. (This is an essay on morale, not morality, and we do not take the position here that good morale is an end in itself or that poor morale is to be avoided at all costs.) Low morale does not lead *inevitably* to costly consequences; but it can do so frequently enough (and severely enough) that the question should be periodically reexamined.

Morale surveys are not the only way, or even necessarily the best way, of conducting such a reexamination. These surveys are valuable primarily when there is a "mystery" to be solved and when the solution (as in the two preceding cases) can pay off handsomely. Mere curiosity is no reason for a morale study, and neither are managerial fashions (which change almost as often as fashions in clothing) or a desire to be modern and sophisticated.

Another worthwhile application of such surveys is to evaluate the effectiveness of policies introduced to affect morale. These are best done at least a year after the policy is put into effect, and they presuppose a previous survey to which comparisons can be made.

Some managers tend to view morale surveys as potential indictments of their own work and for that reason argue that they are unnecessary, unreliable, or even dangerous. They may indeed be all three—but not for that reason. Surveys should not be undertaken without some specific reason, such as resolving an important morale question or establishing a baseline against which to evaluate the effects of some new policy. They can be unreliable when carried out with too small a sample or when too much of the data consist of interviewer's impressions and not enough of the employees' own responses. They can be dangerous when management is not committed to some kind of responsive action, so that expectations are aroused and then neglected.

Indeed, the readiness of management to react constructively to survey results (not the survey methods themselves) is the crucial factor in determining whether a survey should be done at all and whether it is likely to lead to useful results. The following comments, taken from a preliminary "feasibility study" to determine if a morale survey should be made, illustrate some of the more common attitudes of line managers toward the prospect of a morale survey:

I don't feel that I need any third parties to communicate for me. If the intent of your survey is to find out what attitudes are, I can do that just by brainstorming with four or five of my foremen for an hour or so on whatever the hell they want to talk to me about. In fact, I've started doing this about once a month or so. And whenever I hear a rumor— you know, we have some crazy rumors around here sometimes—I call a meeting right away with my foremen, and I squelch it. *Production Superintendent*

I'm a little scared of this survey, to tell you the truth. We know what the problems are: broken windows that don't get fixed, dripping pipes that don't get fixed. The problem is we don't have the money, so we go after the big things and all these little ones just have to wait. But it's the the little things that bother people. You know, like you're the guy standing under the damn pipe and it's your head it's dripping on. I know damn well you'll hear all about housekeeping and safety and maintenance—all of those "motherhood" words. Those are all legitimate gripes, but I'll tell you what scares me: we're going to get a lot of good ideas out of this survey, and then they don't give any money to do anything about them. *Maintenance Manager*

There is a "why bother?" attitude toward this idea for a survey. I mean, we've already told those guys [management] about the problems. There wasn't any result then, so why should we expect a result now? Why would they listen to you if they didn't listen to us? *Shipping Foreman*

I'll tell you what I'd like to know. There is a small, vocal minority that really runs that union. The officers are just figureheads. These are the militants who show up at all the meetings, and all the rest just follow them like sheep. But you talk to these guys one at a time, and they'll tell you they don't like what their union is doing. What I'd like to know is, does the union really speak for its members? Do they know what those guys really want? Are they [the union leadership] just a minority, or do the others really believe what they tell them? *Production Superintendent*

You know what I think? You're going to do your job, interviews and questionnaires and all that. Then the computer is going to do its job. Then you'll make a big presentation to the brass and write a big report. And that's about it. One year from now, nothing is going to be any different. Why should it? What are you going to tell them that they don't already know—that is, if they listen? *Quality Control Manager*

With the exception of the second production superintendent, who saw the survey as an opportunity for valuable insights, most of these managers were saying that the morale problems of their company were already known; and they were expressing doubt that anything more would be done about them after a survey than had been done before. If they were right on either count, a survey would have been pointless. (As it happened, top management disagreed, held the survey anyway, and—motivated in part by the desire to prove that their cynical subordinates had underestimated them—responded energetically to the results.)

When they are properly executed, surveys are elaborate, sophisticated procedures; therefore they should be used only when there is a need for them and when management is prepared to make the adjustments for which the data indicate a need. Most of the time at least one, and more likely both, of these conditions do not exist. Therefore surveys represent a comparatively rare intervention.

But the problem of assessing and responding to morale *always* exists; and fortunately, there are ways of doing this that do not require anything so complex as a survey. They do require a finely tuned ear, however, and above all an appreciation for the importance of what other people are thinking. The art of listening can be taught; but the recognition that listening is indispensable to effective management is a form of wisdom that must be learned (if it is ever learned at all) from the experience of life itself.

The manager with the good sense to listen to what subordinates have to say, and to how they say it, will tend to encounter one of three complaint patterns: healthy complaints, unhealthy complaints, and no complaints at all.

A "healthy" complaint is unlikely to lead to deteriorated morale or costly behavior. It usually expresses the frustration of immediate or momentary, rather then fundamental or permanent, needs. It tends to be concerned with obstacles to getting the job done effectively, such as inferior tools, inadequate maintenance, or unreliable information. The fact that a complaint is unlikely to lead to serious consequences is no reason, of course, for ignoring it. In most cases the employee is seeking the removal of a handicap on productivity, so it is very much to management's own interests to alleviate the problem if it can.

"Unhealthy" complaints can, if not attended to, lead to worsened morale and even to retaliatory behavior. Usually fundamental needs are involved, such as the need to be treated fairly relative to others, the need to be able to affect one's future and to improve one's situation, as well as the more familiar needs for economic security, adequate income, and recognition for one's efforts. Broadly speaking, unhealthy complaints tend to focus on what is given *in exchange for work*—in contrast to healthy complaints, which focus on obstacles *to doing the work*.

Healthy complaints are easy to alleviate but can be safely postponed if necessary—at least as far as morale is concerned. However, unhealthy complaints are frequently difficult to alleviate and demand a prompt response—even if it is only an acknowledgment that the problem exists. The sad paradox is, of course, that the complaints least in need of attention receive it most promptly, while those with the most urgent need are least likely to receive any at all.

The "no complaint" condition is the most difficult of all to deal with, since it has two possible causes and they are diametric opposites. On the one hand, it might imply nothing more than what it looks like: people with no particular problems who are simply going about their business. But it could also result from employees' sullen distrust of management and a corresponding unwillingness to reveal anything, lest it be used to their disadvantage. Such people are usually nursing old, aggravated grievances and are always potentially ripe for a seemingly "sudden" explosion. There is no reliable *superficial* way to tell the two conditions apart—which is why so many managements are taken by complete surprise when previously "docile" employees strike or take some other aggressive action.

The best way to determine whether a "no complaint" condition is really that, or conceals something more sinister, is to consider the group's history. Morale is, after all, a summary of all the psychologically significant events one has experienced within recent memory. Its day-to-day fluctuations, while perhaps dramatic at the moment, are ultimately trivial. What moves it toward extremes is not a specific event but continued patterns of events. Thus one can consider the recent history (say, the past year or two) of an individual or group to determine whether a "no complaint" condition is consistent with tranquility or suppressed anger. Especially if a complaint was once serious enough to be voiced, but is no longer heard even if its cause has not been removed, it would be fatuous in the extreme to assume that the employees have simply "forgotten" about it.

Employees with "unhealthy" complaints are rendering a vitally important service to their boss by telling him or her about it. They relieve their superior of the necessity to surmise that something may be wrong and even of the necessity of diagnosing what is wrong. Employees who keep their complaints to themselves are easier to live with only as long as they continue to do so and may be virtually impossible to live with if they ever give vent to their pent-up feelings. Therefore, complaining employees should never be regarded as a nuisance, even when they are doing their best to make nuisances of themselves.

Once a complaint has surfaced, the most important thing to do is acknowledge it and—within a reasonable time—take some kind of definite position on it. If it can be rectified, fine; if not, it is vital that the employees be told why. One should not expect that they will agree with the explanation, much less that they will enjoy it. Neither are necessary. All that is required is that they understand it. Even when managers and subordinates can only agree to disagree, the results are preferable to not communicating at all. In the last analysis, communication—even when it is contentious—is the best preventive and antidote for poor morale and the best assurance that positive morale can ultimately be attained.

Index